BREAK**THROUGH**
~~**DOWN**~~

TRUE STORY

BREAK~~DOWN~~ THROUGH

SOMETIMES THINGS
HAVE TO FALL APART
TO FALL INTO PLACE

SADIE SHARP

Published in 2019 by Fuzzy Flamingo
Copyright © Sadie Sharp 2019

ISBN: Paperback 978-1-9161147-2-2
ISBN: ebook 978-1-9161147-3-9

Front cover design © Fuzzy Flamingo
A catalogue for this book is available from the
British Library.

Dedicted to Sarah James-Wright, my muse disguised as a coach. Had it not been for you telling me to put my pen and paper down on that first session, and making me cry every time we met since, I 100% would never have had the confidence to step out from under my own shadow and write this book, let alone push ahead with the rest of my U-turn initiatives! Thank you for helping me grow into me.

Acknowledgements

Cassandra Farren – thank you for coaxing me to write this book, and then coaching me on how to do it properly!

My friends and family – thank you for helping me through everything, even when you may have not realised that that's what you were doing.

Andy – thank you for carving out a little piece of writer's heaven in a quiet corner of Bali for me to pour myself into this book in 5 days straight!

Foreword

You should know that if this book ever makes it out into the big bad world, I have no idea whether you'll like it. I have no idea whether *I'll* like it! There will certainly be some people from my past that won't like it.

When you spend the vast majority of your life wanting to write a book about your life, you also find 101 things to stop you from doing so. Like, what if I upset the people that I talk about by sharing my story?; What will happen when I share something that the people close to me still don't even know happened?; What if nobody reads it?

I mean, I'm a normal person doing normal things, going through normal shit. Right?

Well, apparently not… On the odd occasion when I do lift my Fort Knox-style emotional walls and open up to someone about my life, their jaw drops and they say, "You should SOOOO write a book!" So, here I am… despite being the grand old age of 36, and still wondering what possible right do I have to write a book?!?

I'm currently sat on my friend's sofa in Portugal, where I've been squatting for the past week in an attempt to forcibly extract myself from the world long enough to try and find the words to explain my journey – partly for my benefit, so that I can feel more at peace with my life and who I am now as a result of it; but mainly for you. For the you who you are today, for the you who you used to be, and for the you who you could become… if only you can make it through this day/week/month/year, and lurch towards a life that bears more pleasure than pain. More joy than suffering. More hope than regret.

As I see it, life has a tendency (in the words of Steve Jobs) to hit you in the head with a brick! Sometimes once, sometimes several times over. And the only thing that makes the difference between whether we break and heal, or break and shatter, is our ability to take lessons from everything that happens to us. But those lessons don't all need to be learnt by us and us alone. So, I'm sharing with you not just my story, but the lessons that I learnt along the way.

This book is for the person who feels broken inside, but presents a coat of armour to the world that would make an armadillo look like a walking marshmallow.

This book is for the person that spends years striving to create the life they want, and then one day wakes up to feel like they're the only inmate in a prison of their very own making.

This book is for the person who knows the dark depths of life and longs for a glimmer of light to reveal the emergency exit.

This book is for the person who life hits in the head with a brick and who then doesn't know what the fuck to do with all the bricks at their feet.

And this book is for the person that loses their rock, their role model, their north star, and tries to not lose their shit while they rebuild their life.

Enjoy ☺

(PS – sorry not sorry for swearing. My mum once told me I was like a little lady with the vocabulary of a sailor, and I write as I speak. So, hopefully you can forgive me for being me.)

CHAPTER 1

Broken

I was curled up on my sofa, tightly coiled in the foetal position. Wrapped up in a tatty, grey fleece blanket, I wriggled my arm out to wipe my nose with a crinkled piece of toilet roll. My dog Mia wandered over and gently licked one of the tears streaming down my face, and I rolled over to avoid her doing the same with the snot streaming out of my nose. I love my dog, but that's a step too far.

As I rolled over in-between my sobs, I was grateful for the temporary break from the view of the permanently drawn curtains and stacked brown removal boxes that I hadn't even bothered to clear from the dining table.

I wanted out. I wanted to get off. I wanted anything but to be me in my life right then. I felt like I had spent that past few years of my life stacking more and more coal into a steam-train to make it go faster and faster, and had just realised that the brakes don't work and the tracks I'd laid down were taking me somewhere I didn't want to go. And that I didn't even fucking like trains.

I was a blubbering mess, and I struggled to reconcile it with the person I had been just 24 hours before. I was fine – or so I kept telling myself. I was managing my two businesses, mentoring teenagers, doing pro-bono work with charities, financially floating the majority of my family, travelling the globe to consult for huge companies, and was just a few months away from my departure to climb Mount Everest.

I was more successful than I had ever thought was possible. Yet here I was, struggling to get off the sofa.

I pulled my knees in closer to my chest and let out a few more uncontrollable sobs, still reeling from my trip to the doctor's earlier that day. It's funny how one conversation can have the same impact on your life as a category 5 earthquake can on an unsuspecting town.

I was at the peak of my game. I was a 31-year-old management consultant, had started my own company at the age of 24, then gone on to start up several other companies, employ staff, and throw myself at everything life had to offer. I had recently had a Nike Year where "Just Do It" had been my chosen life motto. I had (literally) crammed in everything that I'd been putting off until I had more time or money, or whatever other excuses we tell ourselves to delay living our lives as fully as we could if we get out of our own way (more on that later). So, my already busy life had become even more busy, which had also been compounded by the fact that I had just moved twice inside 12 months.

But that day had started out like any other. I was preparing for my trip to Everest, so was up at 4am to do a couple of hours training in the gym before jumping onto a couple of conference calls, shooting out a few emails, juggling a few meetings round for later in the week, sending out invoices for work done, booking a hotel and flights for my last work gig before going away, taking my mum to the supermarket, moving my brother out of his flat, checking in with my staff, and grabbing a sandwich on my way to the doctor's to get some altitude sickness tablets for my expedition.

In the waiting room at the doctor's, I sent off a few more emails on my phone, and moved around a few of the overstuffed commitments in my diary like I was playing Tetris, optimising my time down to the millisecond.

I heard my name called and looked up at a friendly looking blonde lady in her 40s. I followed her and her swishy blue skirt into the consulting room, and sat on the waterproofed nylon chair while she opened up my notes and said, "So, how can I help?"

"I'm climbing Everest in a couple of months, and apparently I need altitude sickness tablets," I said in a matter of fact, business-like tone.

"Oh, blimey," she said, "that's brave! Do you do a lot of mountaineering?"

"No, not at all," I replied with a wry smile, "but I like a challenge, so I've been training really hard."

This time, my tone was matter of fact, but I could feel my suppressed sense of panic starting to rise as my voice broke slightly and a hollow smile became pasted to my face. But it was my eyes that gave me away; I felt them filling up with tears. I started to say, "I'm ok really, but I do have a lot on at the moment, so maybe you could give me something to help me cope?" And that was that. I was inconsolably sobbing in-between my muffled attempts to say "I'm sorry" and "I'm OK really", as though saying it again and again might actually convince either of us that it was true.

"OK," she said, with that neutrally professional tone that doctors perfect to cover their rising concern at the state unravelling in front of their eyes. "Tell me a bit more about what's going on in your life right now," she said encouragingly. I didn't even know where to begin, so I just blurted it all out, in no order at all.

After reeling off the crazy commitments that I'd crammed into my life, I took a big breath of resigned acceptance. It was all out there now – I'd cracked the lid open just a tiny bit, and it all came bursting out like a Jack-in-the-Box stuffed with self-made grenades. "I feel trapped. I feel like I'm a robot on autopilot. I'm functioning on the outside, and everybody thinks I'm fine. Hell, I fake it so well even I think I'm fine most of the time. But all I see around me is obligations, and commitments, and challenges, and struggles... and I can't push the panic down any more. I'm not fine. I can't cope, and I don't know what to do about it."

While the tears streamed down my face and the doctor sat there empathetically, I finished by voicing the one fear I had spent whatever energy I had left denying to myself. "And... on top of all of that, I think that the love of my life is about to leave me," I said, letting out a silent wail that expelled whatever life I might have had left in me.

"OK. I need you to fill out this little questionnaire," she told me, sliding a small sheet of paper across the desk towards me. I sniffed as I ticked boxes, asking on a scale of 1-5 a range of questions on how unhappy I was, how often I cried, and how often I thought about taking my own life. I slid my responses back toward her and, apart from having never considered suicide, all of my answers were resoundingly down the unhealthy end of the scale.

Even to this day, I can still recall her words clear as day. "I think you have depression as a result of the severe stress that you've been under, and I think you might be having a breakdown. The last thing you need is to be going up the world's highest mountain."

I nodded my head. I knew she was right, and the thought had crossed my mind, but I'd told myself it was just self-doubt and fear, two of the things that I prided myself on not giving into. The doctor said a few things that passed in a bit of a blur – I think there was an analogy about handling pressure and depression, but I wasn't really listening. I nodded numbly as she booked me an appointment with the practice psychologist the following week, and gave me a prescription for Prozac.

I left the doctor's surgery 45 minutes later, and made my way home in a daze. Ever since then, I have been rather more sympathetic when doctors overrun and are late for their appointments, because I was one of those people who just couldn't cram all of my shit into the scheduled ten minutes.

I had also used up the majority of the box of Kleenex on the doctor's table, so my eyes looked like something out of a horror movie when I walked into the pharmacy, head down, hoping to God that I didn't bump into anyone I knew. I collected my prescription, and curled up in the foetal position as soon as I got home, which is where we started this chapter.

I was starting to doze off on the sofa when I heard my phone ping. I turned over and picked it up.

TEXT FROM NOAH: *I'm going back to Joan. I'm sorry.*

Those seven words made my stomach lurch into my throat. The darkness surrounding me just plummeted to a new level of blackness as the shocked numbness set in, sprinkled with a light dusting of self-deprecation and a side order of rage. I knew it. Why the fuck did I go there? I'm an idiot for thinking it would be any different this time around. No wonder he left, I'm a fucking nutjob. But what a fucking asshole! How fucking dare he do this by text. YOU FUCKING COWARD! That's it – I'm done. I will only ride this merry-go-round so many times. FUCK YOU!

TEXT TO NOAH: *I never want to see or hear from you again.*

I set my phone back down on the table and laughed at myself. That really told him, didn't it?! Always trying to be the bigger person, eh? That was about as aggressively

British as it is to leave the word 'Regards' off an email when you're pissed off at someone.

Then the numbness settled in again like a familiar heavy blanket of snow, so I dragged myself off the sofa and stumbled towards my bedroom. I felt like my insides had just been ripped out and stuffed down my throat. I crawled into bed and stared at my bedside alarm clock. It was only 4pm. No need to draw the curtains, as they hadn't been open for days now anyway. I dumped my bag on the floor and blinked as my gaze re-focused on the little white stick that fell out, and the two purple lines showing on the dial. A positive pregnancy test. Because things weren't quite shite enough as they were.

Life had just hit me in the head with a brick.

★ ★ ★

Before I give you the wrong impression – this isn't a book about a broken love story or the one that got away. Don't get me wrong, I *was* heartbroken, and there was much more to this part of the story (which I'll go into later), but my break-up wasn't what broke me.

I WAS ALREADY BROKEN.

I was just holding it together, so desperately trying to prove to myself that I could cope that I forgot to ask myself whether I actually wanted to cope any more. This break-up was just the straw that broke the camel's back. It was the tipping point that I NEEDED to starkly review where I had taken my life, and to honestly question whether it was healthy, sustainable, and what I actually wanted.

Now, I'm not recommending that people aim to have a breakdown (!), because you certainly don't need to take things to breaking point before asking these questions of yourself. But in hindsight, I can now recognise that I only got to that point because I didn't recognise the steps I'd taken that contributed to my state of mind. I didn't recognise the emotional strain that unresolved issues caused me when trying to push them deep, deep down inside. And I didn't understand myself well enough to see when I was the one destroying me.

Over my life there have been a jigsaw of moments which made me. And each of those moments carry meaning for me and my life. Some good, some bad, some indifferent. Some I saw, some I didn't, and some I closed my eyes to.

It's those moments that I will share with you. But to make sense of it all, we need to go back to the beginning...

CHAPTER LESSONS:

- Sometimes it takes being hit in the head with a brick to knock some fucking sense into you.
- There are times in life when not getting what you want is the best thing to ever happen to you. You just rarely know it at the time.

CHAPTER 2

A Good Start

My memory is terrible. I mean catastrophically short-term, to the point where I can only align it to a computer hard drive that is full and keeps popping up with the 'unable to save file due to insufficient memory' notice. But my brain doesn't issue pop-up notices, so you never quite know what will go in and be available for retrieval at a later date and what is gone forever as if it never happened!

So, writing a chapter on my early years is a bit of a challenge. However, the advantage that this affliction presents is that the only things that I can actually recall are the things that are the most buoyant and meaningful of memories. Yet I do so with a distinct caveat.

You see, it has been in my most recent years that a series of events and decisions (writing this book being one of them) led me to see my childhood events in a different light. As we all grow up, we see our lives through the eyes of a child, as an adolescent, and as an adult, experiencing our events in the first person – with our own views, opinions, and baggage influencing the meaning that we attach to what we see happening before us.

However, it's not until our later years (if ever!) that we start to un-learn some of the things that we took as gospel when growing up. And we often change our opinions of our parents when we finally see past their role as the expectedly perfect parent to the fallible adults they really are, with their own baggage, issues, and struggles, making it up as they go along, doing the best they can, hoping they don't completely fuck it up!

And I'm sure mine probably thought they came close a couple of times, but I don't think they fucked it up at all.

My earliest childhood memory is of me and my brother playing dress-up at a family friend's house. I must have been about seven or eight, and was a princess with a pretty pink dress. I had decided that my little brother Rhys, who was three years my junior, would be a pirate, so I'd strapped his leg up behind him, tied a tea-towel on his head, and taped a folded-up piece of toilet paper over his eye as a makeshift eye patch. I dragged my one-legged little brother into the lounge to show our mother.

"I'm going to run a play about Peter Pan, and Rhys will be the pirate, and I will be the princess," I announced confidently, with my hands placed firmly on my waist.

My mother put down her large glass of Liebfraumilch wine and said, "Darling, I'm not sure there is a princess in *Peter Pan*. Maybe you mean you want to be Wendy, or Tinker Bell the fairy?"

"Well there will be a princess in my version of *Peter*

Pan," I declared indignantly! I never was one for doing things by the rule book, and my stubborn tenacity was clearly present from an early age. No wonder my mother drank!

My propensity for creating things, launching projects, and generally bossing people around definitely started at a young age. I would always be directing a play or choreographing a new dance routine with the other kids when at my childminder's, who was also our next-door neighbour. Mary would pick us up from junior school and look after us until Mum finished work. We were there frequently, because Mum had a few different jobs and Dad worked away a lot, so I was comfortable having what I considered to be adult conversations with Mary.

I remember designing a cheerleading outfit at primary school one day and asking Mary whether she thought I should design it in yellow and blue, or red and blue, only for her to tell me that yellow and blue might be a bit clashy. In true-to-self style, I responded with, "Well, that is the whole point, silly. That's ok – I'll figure it out myself." That poor woman must have gritted her teeth more times than she cares to remember!

Despite having some very strong opinions on the world, I wasn't one of those kids that had big aspirations about what they wanted to do when they grew up. I did ok at school, but never set the world on fire with any noticeable capabilities or inspiring ambitions. I went with the flow of the current, as did most other emerging teens. I was approaching age 11, and watching a TV series about deep sea adventures (which also happened to feature my first celebrity crush), when I decided I wanted to be a marine biologist. I also kinda liked dolphins, so it seemed like a sensible idea for me at the time.

It also gave my dad something to focus on when bringing little gifts when he returned from working away. Even to this day, I still come across the occasional tiny statue of a pair of dolphins jumping a ceramic tidal crest, or a small stuffed toy seal. I remember that I loved seeing Dad come home – partly for the gift I knew he would have, but also because we rarely saw him during the week. He often had to travel round the UK and Europe as part of his sales job, which put a clear strain on his relationship with Mum. I guess they tried to strike a balance on the weekends by splitting family time and social time, with me and my brother chowing down on a pizza, packet of crisps, and a half a coke in the back room of various pubs around the little town where we lived outside Swindon. Even though my mum would later tell me that she hated us spending so much time in pubs when growing up, to this day they are some of my fondest memories. I felt like we were sharing a little bit of their adult world... and the pizzas were awesome!

Aside from these moments, I'm sad to say that I have very few memories of my dad while growing up. Besides the time in the back room of a pub, and the occasional swimming trip that was often the result of a post-argument, making-up gesture to my mother, my only other memories are of my dad on the sofa on a Sunday afternoon, eating his re-heated Sunday lunch, watching a black and white spaghetti western movie on the TV, with me and my brother sat either side of him. Mum would have fed us our lunch hours earlier, while he was at the Rugby Club doing first aid for the games, or catching up with his fellow committee members. He was a social being, and Mum would say years later that he was too much of a forever bachelor to have had children. However, in my recent adult years, I realise that he was just doing the best he could.

The recession had hit my parents hard, and they had to take out a second mortgage on the house. Dad took on more work to earn more money, but that meant more time away from his family. That put a strain on their marriage, which meant that time at home became less and less of a haven, so he spent less time there and more time in the places where he could numb the pain of what must have become a very difficult life.

Our holidays were a brief respite from our usual routine, but Mum hated flying, so we usually went camping. The site was of course chosen for its geographical proximity to a local pub, but that aside, my brother and I spent many a day rock-pooling to find crabs. We'd take them back to the tent in a bucket of water, only to find them gone hours later, then we'd spend the rest of the holiday worrying that they would crawl into our tent and vengefully snip our toes off in the middle of the night. It was only years later that Mum admitted to us that she would return them to the rocks when we were distracted, yet let us fret as a deterrent to keep bringing them back. Our nights there were filled with endless games of cards. Mum would polish off a bottle of wine teaching me and Rhys new card games, while we waited for Dad to come home from his early evening drink at the pub.

Aside from our holidays, and the back room of pubs, the only other memories I have of my parents together is of them arguing. I don't remember what was said, just of sitting at the top of the stairs at night crying as I listened to them screaming at each other. One time, I assume an argument made it into the next day, as Mum roped us into playing a joke on Dad where we put flour into a bucket and balanced it on top of the lounge door, so when he came in (I assume much later than he should have) he got covered in flour. My brother and I thought it was hilarious, of course, but I see now that it was one of the many dysfunctional incidents in my parents' marriage.

But as with all things in life, their marriage wasn't one-sided. Mum had had two children in her first marriage. But when they divorced, her first husband moved to South Africa to live – and one day, he omitted to return the two young boys back to the UK after their holiday to visit him had finished. After years of searching, strained communications, and severely damaged emotional ties, the boys grew up in South Africa, and didn't return to the UK until years later, when my mother had married my father and had just had me and my brother.

As you can imagine, this caused an unimaginable amount of damage to my mother and to the boys, much of which no doubt still lingers today. When the boys did eventually make their way back to the UK and attempted to rebuild a relationship with their mother, my father welcomed them with open arms, moving them in and helping them find college courses and jobs. And there were many years where the childminding duties fell to our older brothers, who would tickle us until we would concede and admit to where Mum had stashed the bag of chocolate!

On one such an occasion, I was searching for said stash of chocolate when I reached inside the tumble dryer and my hand landed on a half empty bottle of gin. I was about 12 at the time and thought nothing of it as it wasn't the chocolate I was looking for, but speaking to my father in recent years, it was one of many that he would find stashed around the house. It appears that my mother also had her vices to numb the pain; hers were just consumed more at home than away.

Just before I turned 13, my parents sat us down and told us that they were splitting up. My mum had met someone else, and would be moving out with us. I said some truly horrible things to her, which I still feel bad about to this day. Looking back through adult eyes, I can see that they were both in a relationship that must have been destroying who they were. And to this day, my father is still mortally wounded at how the split and subsequent years played out.

My mum did leave for someone else, but it didn't last long. So, after about 18 months, we moved into social housing and she took on a second job to help make ends meet while I finished sixth form and my brother completed his GCSEs. As the years progressed, my mother stayed on her own, never even having a single date, and it was my father who re-married. Despite their broken relationship and inability to tolerate each other for more than a few minutes of passing conversation about myself and my brother, they always worked together to ensure that we wanted for nothing. Mum invested 200% of her attention on us and Dad supported us financially wherever possible, making sure we made it through college and university.

And despite this blip in our developmental history, I think we both turned out pretty well in the end.

Apart from, maybe, my incessant drive to grow up and take on the world before my time. In an early grab at independence, when I turned 15 I took a job stacking shelves at a local shop, and would go there after school each day for a couple of hours to earn some money to spend on clothes (and the occasional bottle of 20:20 that I would smuggle over to a friend's house to drink!).

It was in this job that I met Donny, my 25-year-old boss, who treated me like a proper adult, showing me how to manage the stock, cash up the till, and work the computer… whilst I sat on his lap. Within a couple of months of working there, he told me that I could be his girlfriend, if I wanted. I was, of course, flattered that an older guy was interested in little old me, and the whole situation made me feel *very* mature…

The following week, I told my mum I was working late one night to do a stock-check, and went round his house for dinner. I had two glasses of wine and ended up losing my virginity. It was horrible, but I told myself that it's what adults did, so brushed off the sentiment and puffed up my chest. At work, we fooled around in the stock room, away from prying eyes, because he said he "didn't want to make anyone else jealous". And I was hooked.

It was the first time I'd ever had male attention, and I wanted to tell my mum all about it. So, I did…

"I'm dating my boss, and he's 25, and we're having sex, and you can't stop me so don't even try!" My mother's face drained of colour. She got up to top up her glass of wine, lit a cigarette, and took a long hard drag. After what felt like an age, she let out a heavy sigh. I can't remember exactly what she said, but I remember that it wasn't the protest I was expecting. She thanked me for telling her, said that she didn't like the idea, but was glad that she knew. She would rather I didn't see him, but if I was going to do it anyway, she wouldn't stop me – her only request was that I always told her where I was.

Donny and I continued to 'date' (in his flat) for another couple of months, but I found another job (discreetly facilitated by my mother) and things fizzled out. Although this man's intentions were not sinister by today's standards (and looking back, I think he was actually a little bit sad!), nonetheless I do recognise that I was groomed.

I can see that this wasn't the response many mothers would have given, but I guess she knew I was stubborn enough to do what I was set on, so she would rather be kept in the loop than drive me underground. What is interesting is that her reaction to this situation – right, wrong, or otherwise – proved to be pivotal in shifting the dynamics of our relationship. This was the founding moment of our new unshakeable adolescent:parent bond that we would go on to have well into my 30s, where I would tell her everything and speak to her almost every day, even throughout university. Her treating me as an adult who was capable of making my own decisions (even though she might be working to change the situation in the background!) made me feel like there was nothing I couldn't tell her.

Although this would go on to face the ultimate test in my first year of university…

CHAPTER LESSONS:

- How you want to react to a situation, and the reaction that will get you the best outcome, are often poles apart. When choosing between them, consider the long-term impact of the outcome. Had my mother reacted differently to my relationship, I would have carried on anyway and started a trend of hiding things from her. Had this become the case, I genuinely don't think I would have been able to turn to her when the shit hit the fan in later years.

• When we are growing up, we look at the world through our eyes, and our eyes alone. The things we see influence what we think about the people around us, and we form beliefs and expectations about them and about ourselves. Then we grow up, and our view of the world expands. We evolve into more educated, understanding, and emotionally intelligent adults who see the world for what it is and our parents as the fallible adults they are. However, those early formed beliefs are often so engrained that we don't notice when they don't always evolve with us, and if you're not careful they can screw up your life navigation like holding a magnet next to a compass.

CHAPTER 3

Donna & Nigel

Growing up, we had quite a small family unit where Mum and Dad had moved away from Wales and relocated in Swindon. But despite the distance, Mum and Dad had always been close with Donna and Nigel from their days of living in Wales, and we spent a lot of time with them when growing up.

Apparently Mum and Donna became friends when they were in their early twenties and thirties (Mum was 10 years older) where Donna got drunk one night in a pub and rambled on to my heavily pregnant mother about her shitty upbringing, where her mum had decided to move to London to follow a succession of unsuitable men rather than bring up her own child, leaving Donna to be raised by her extended family.

But despite her shaky start in life, Donna had a sensible head on her shoulders, and she had landed a job, bought herself a place, met a nice guy called Nigel, and crafted a decent life for herself.

My mother had a knack of sniffing out a rescue case from 15 yards across a crowded room, and meeting Donna was no exception. From that moment onwards they were pretty much inseparable, with my mum taking it upon herself to act as an unofficial interfering mother figure at every opportunity.

So, when Mum and Dad started out life as parents in Wales, the tables would turn and Donna would take me and my brother out whilst on her early dates with Nigel. And later, when we moved to Swindon, I remember countless weekends where my parents would drive me and Rhys to the Severn Bridge to hand us over to Donna and Nigel halfway, so that they could have a weekend off parenting! This surrogate parenting relationship carried on well into my teens after my parents had split up, with me, Rhys, and Mum visiting Wales for a weekend, and Mum dropping us off at Donna's to go and visit friends. I usually played hairdresser and spent the weekend brushing her long hair and carrying her shopping bags on our frequent trips to the city centre, while Rhys would go out with Nigel to play golf or help him do magic at kids' discos in the evenings.

I wanted to be like Donna when I grew up – she was pretty, had a good job, bought cool clothes, and had the prefect relationship where they went on holiday what seemed like every other month! Rhys saw Nigel as a role model, and was resolute that he would one day become a magician himself. At some point over the years, both my parents agreed that if anything were to happen to them, then me and Rhys would go to live with Donna and Nigel. Our surrogate, back-up parents had been chosen.

So, when it came time for me to make the decision

about which university to go to, it made sense for me to go to one in Wales, as Donna and Nigel were nearby to ensure that I got fed and watered, and Donna's ironing lady would save me a few trips to the uni laundry room! I accepted a place at law school and eagerly packed as much useless shit as I could into my father's estate car, and trundled across the bridge to Wales in early September 2000.

As we arrived at my accommodation halls, I unpacked my array of pink feather boas, ultra-trendy lava lamps, and a collection of stuffed toys that would make most five-year-olds jealous, and met one of my new housemates – Becky. I would go on to live with for the rest of my time in university, and later became godmother to her children.

As expected, I spent the majority of the first couple of months shit-faced – at one point tripping over, breaking my fall with my face and chipping my front tooth, which made it even harder to brush off dodgy 'blonde' jokes! And when I ran out of money in-between my grant cheques, I would take my laundry basket over to Donna's for a home-cooked meal and a fully-funded night drinking in their local pub. I had met a great group of friends, my social life was buzzing, I had the perfect safety net in Donna and Nigel, and I'd figured out from my first few lectures that I could still just about follow what the lecturers were saying when I rocked up still half pissed from the night before.

Life was good!

One of the perks of going to university in Wales was that whenever the rugby was on, the whole country was buzzing. So, one Saturday in November, there was a big rugby match on, along with a Remembrance Day silence. I decided to go over to Donna's that afternoon/evening as the pubs around town would have been rammed, and she and Nigel were having a house party that night.

I was never great with girlie small talk, so I'd extracted myself from the group of Donna's friends who were discussing nail-varnish shades and holiday destinations and decided to become a self-elected honorary member of the boys' club next to the bar. I squeezed in next to Nigel, and before I knew it he was passing me a bottle of Reef with a knowing wink.

"Go on, Sades, show 'em what you've learnt at university so far!" he said, and I gladly obliged, demonstrating my self-proclaimed party trick of 'straw-pedo-ing' the bottle down in one long gulp. The night progressed as expected, with me, a 5ft fuck all, petite, 19-year-old 1st year student attempting to keep up with a group of burly blokes, and ending up a stumbling mess by the time we all made our way back to the house for the after party.

I knew how to make an impression, just not a very good one! By this point, I'd decided that I was utterly irresistible, and had started to (attempt to) flirt with one of Nigel's friends, so Donna very wisely decided to put me to bed to sober up a bit. She guided me upstairs to her room in their little cottage, with me sliding along the wall up the stairs.

I flopped into bed and drifted into a deep state of unconsciousness as Donna pulled the covers over me.

* * *

I'm pulled out of my drink-induced, coma-like state by the weight of someone climbing into bed behind me. I dismiss it as Donna retiring for the night while I drift back into my dreamless state. But I wake with a start as I feel someone pulling down my leggings and thrusting their hands into my underwear. *Cheeky fucker*, I think to myself, as I drunkenly attempt to turn over and wriggle away, assuming it to be the guy I was flirting with at the bar.

Then I see that it's Nigel.

I freeze as I try and process what's happening. He's tugging my leggings down and I feel paralysed. There are so many fuzzy thoughts racing through my mind too fast for me to grab onto any of them to figure out what to do.

"No, don't!" I manage to mumble feebly.

He pulls his hands away as he says, "I always thought you fancied me." Then he gets up and leaves, and I drift back off into my drunken coma, hoping that it was all a bad dream.

Nigel came into my bed five times that night, each time progressing his actions, and each time my drunken state gradually reduced so that my head cleared enough to take action. The last time he visited, I learned that he is well hung, and the only reason he didn't manage to take it quite as far as he tried was because he was too drunk to get the angle right from behind.

"GET OFF ME!" I managed to say with more clarity and conviction than before, and he disappeared once again.

I HAVE GOT TO GET OUT OF THIS BED! I thought to myself. So, I slid off the side of the bed and landed in a heap on the floor. The room was spinning as I scrambled to correct my clothing and lurch towards the bedroom door, using the bed to steady myself. I sat on the top step of the stairs for what felt like a lifetime, hoping to God that someone other than Nigel came up the stairs next. I watched a few people come out of the kitchen to use the bathroom at the bottom of the stairs, while the tears silently rolled down my face.

Then I saw the familiar head of blonde hair I was praying for, and I called out to Donna. She came up the stairs with a confused look on her face and guided me back into the bedroom.

"What's wrong?" she said, as she sat next to me on the bed I had just tried so hard to get away from. I sobbed heavily as I tried to find the words. *What the fuck should I say? Would she even believe me?* I wasn't even sure I knew what had just happened, nevertheless try and explain it to someone else.

Even to this day, I still have no idea what I said to her. What words I used to describe what he did. But I remember her response as clear as day. She firmly took my upper arms in her hands and turned me to face her straight-on, then said, "Did he have sex with you?"

I sobbed yet again and looked down, shaking my head. "No. He tried, but no."

The next hour was a bit of a blur, but she collected my bag of stuff from the bedroom, took me back to my room in halls, and then returned to the house party. I curled up in the foetal position in my room for the next couple of days, only coming out to make an occasional bowl of cereal.

I was reeling; I felt like everything I had known had just been turned on its head. I had no idea how to process this or how I was supposed to feel.

I tried to call Donna the week after, but she never picked up. I finally received a text asking me to see her the following weekend. I agreed, as I was yearning for someone to talk to about what had happened. She picked me up the following Saturday… and took me back to the house.

"Nigel wants to apologise," she said, as I sat on the sofa in stunned silence. "Is that ok?"

I nodded my head numbly. *I guess if she can get over it, then maybe I should be able to*, I thought to myself as she went to get Nigel from the kitchen. He wandered into the lounge looking like a repentant schoolboy, with his head down and a sombre look on his face.

I can't remember what he said exactly. Something about being very drunk and not meaning to scare me. And that it wouldn't happen again. Then he looked at Donna, and she tipped her head as if to urge him to continue. Then he said, "I'm sorry" and bent down and hugged me.

In that moment, that hug almost hurt more than what had already happened. I was as rigid as a mannequin, staring ahead, out of the window, wishing I was anywhere other than here. *Does this mean that it's all ok now? Am I supposed to forget what happened? Is Donna ok with this? WHAT THE FUCK IS GOING ON?!?*

As Donna drove me back to halls, she explained that I had nothing to be ashamed of. "Sometimes horrible things in life happen," she said, "but the best way to get over them is to move on."

When I asked her whether I was allowed to tell anyone, she told me I could tell whoever I liked as I'd not done anything wrong. And that she was there for me if I needed her.

I got out of the car, and she waved as she drove off.

★ ★ ★

A few weeks passed and I was operating on autopilot. I attended lectures, saw friends down the pub, and drank. I struggled with social interactions, because I couldn't manage small talk – I felt like I had this huge 'thing' inside me that I didn't know how to process, and until my brain could figure that out, it wasn't able to string together a decent conversation. So, I usually sat quietly in the corner, drinking, while everyone else went about their normal lives.

I dodged calls from my mother and made excuses about going home. She's like a human lie detector when it comes to getting the truth out of people – she just KNOWS when you're hiding something, and deploys more effective cross-examination techniques than interrogators at Guantanamo Bay. But I couldn't possibly tell her. Donna was like a daughter to her, and Nigel was in her fucking will, for God's sake. Rhys would be devastated, and it would ruin her relationship with Donna. I just needed to get over it; Donna seemed to have.

In an attempt to fool myself into thinking that I was getting over it, I went back to the scene of the crime when Donna invited me to her local to have a few drinks with her friends. I accepted, checking that Nigel was away on some kind of business trip. I sat in the pub watching Donna be as fun-filled and bubbly as ever. I struggled to paste on a smile, so moved away to talk to Jim, the son of one of her friends.

We made small talk for a while, and then a tear dropped out of my eye and rolled down my cheek. I wiped it away and saw Donna quickly move towards us. She smiled widely at Jim, handing him a tenner for a round of drinks. As he was at the bar, she turned to me with a concerned frown replacing her smile, and asked, "What are you talking about?"

"Nothing much – just uni stuff," I replied, sniffing.

"Ok," she said, returning to her seat with a quizzical look on her face.

James came back with the drinks and we continued our conversation, but the thoughts in my head started to turn. She hadn't said it explicitly, but the undertone was clear. She told me that I don't have anything to be ashamed of, and that I could tell anyone I like... so long as it didn't impinge on her world and taint this managed reality she had created.

In that moment, something inside me shifted. This woman who was my role model, this woman who I wanted to be like when I grew up... was a fraud. She was a fake. Everything I had seen whilst growing up fell away in one swift, defining moment. I had known for years that she hadn't been happy in her relationship and had been seeing other people, but she had decided to stay, even after this had happened, because of the life she had built. It was easier to stick to what you knew, and benefit from the niceties that your farce afforded you, than it was to start afresh and deal with the shit realities that life presents you with.

I finished my drink and left, crying myself to sleep that night in a quiet rage. My numbness had progressed to anger. I was angry at Donna. I was angry that she was staying with Nigel. I was angry that my role model was no longer a role model. I was furious that she was trying to hide what had happened when I wanted to shout it from the rooftops to get some kind of a sense check from someone other than Donna as to how I should be feeling. I knew that whatever was going on inside me was most definitely not congruent with "getting over it".

The rest of November passed, and December started, with everyone gearing up for the festive season. I, however, was full of dread, as I had finally run out of excuses to avoid going home.

★ ★ ★

I walked into my house and was greeted by a huge smile and hug from my mother. Inside, I wanted to cry and fall apart in her arms, but smiled and laughed on the outside. Then my brother came up behind her and threw his arms around me in a bear hug. And I instantly stiffened. It was as if I was back on Donna's sofa and it was Nigel hugging me again. FUCK. I smiled and patted him on the back, forcibly extracting myself from his embrace with a jibe about his latest fashion *faux pas*.

The next few weeks passed in a blur, with me avoiding deep and meaningful conversations with my mum, drinking way too much, and avoiding any kind of physical contact with my brother or dad. The week before Christmas came, I was doing the annual ritual of wrapping my mum and brother's presents in the lounge, while she packed mine in the kitchen.

She came through with something wrapped up in a plastic bag. "Do you want one of your presents early?" she asked.

My mum was a terrible receiver when it came to gifts, but she LOVED giving. She was as impatient as a five-year-old child when trying to maintain a surprise, making it a mandatory responsibility to open at least one of our presents before Christmas Day.

I laughed and said, "Well, it would be unfair of me to make you wait until Christmas Day, wouldn't it?"

She smiled and came and sat beside me on the sofa, placing the bag in my lap. I reached into the bag and pulled it out. It was a beautiful framed photo from one of the rugby club balls we had attended a few years earlier.

"I thought you could put it up in your dorm room?" she suggested. The picture was of me and Rhys, and Donna and Nigel.

I sucked my lips inside, biting them together in an attempt to force a smile and hold back the tears, but it didn't work. I burst into tears and couldn't stop sobbing. I have no recollection of what I told my mother that day, but I remember the look on her face. The look of utter shock, of bitter disappointment, and a flash of rage that I think never actually left her.

We sat up for hours talking, and I agreed to go to the doctor's the next day to get some counselling. In bed that night, my feelings lurched from relief that it would all be ok now that Mum knew, to *Oh my God, I opened Pandora's box and now I can't take it back!*

From what I gather from later conversations, my mother spent the night on the phone calling round everyone concerned like it was some kind of national emergency. She spoke to Donna, she told my father, and apparently she spoke to Nigel. I have no idea what was said to any of them, but the next few days came and went. The one conversation I do remember – and still brings tears to my eyes to this very day – is when she told my brother Rhys. He was 16 at the time, and as she explained in basic detail what happened, you could see the look of confusion on his face turn into a mix of protective sympathy and vengeful rage. He turned to me and said, "It's ok, Sades, I'll look after you." Then he pulled me into a big hug. I tried not to noticeably stiffen as I hugged him back and wiped away my tears over his shoulder.

What Mum said to get me a next day doctor's appointment and a counselling session the following week, I have no idea. But I only ended up having two counselling sessions. At some point in the second session, I came out with, "I understand it, but I don't respect it." And I realised that the turmoil I was struggling with around Donna and the fact that she had stayed wasn't because I didn't understand it or disagreed with it. I COMPLETELY understood why. Her mother had left her, and the only stability she knew was Nigel. Although by anyone else's standards, it wasn't a healthy relationship, she needed it. Despite what had happened, she couldn't bring herself to walk away and start again. And THAT was what I hated. I had lost respect for the one person that I wanted to be like 'when I grew up'. Yes, I obviously was upset as a result of what Nigel did, but the bit I struggled with the most was the way that Donna had handled the situation. I understood it, but I didn't respect it.

And that was it – it felt like something had clicked

into place, and my head was a bit clearer. We fumbled through Christmas, and I returned to Uni. I would still swing all over the place with my emotions over the next couple of years, being angry at Donna one minute, almost blaming her for what happened, to the next minute asking her to go for lunch to try and rekindle the relationship that we used to have. I tried on a few occasions to talk to her about what happened, but she refused, not wanting to "go over what is behind us because you can't change what's happened". Eventually, I gave up and played along.

I managed to graduate from university nonetheless, and a couple of years later Donna (who had finally left Nigel when she met someone else) invited me and Rhys to Spain on holiday for her 40th birthday. I had less and less contact with her over the years as life got busy and our unresolved issues always felt like we were playing at happy families when we did occasionally meet up. So I was looking forward to being able to spend time with her around other people, which would allow our slightly awkward dynamic to be somewhat diluted.

In the middle of the week we all went out to a bar and were on the drunk side of sober. I was having a conversation with Donna's new partner, saying how nice it was that she seemed so happy and was seeing someone that was so normal, especially after what had happened. Despite the fact that they had been together for quite some time by then, he had absolutely no idea about what had happened.

I was outraged. I could almost understand not wanting other people who were a part of your life back then to know about what happened, but she hadn't even shared it with her new partner. I could only assume it was a part of why she and Nigel had broken up, yet was the sole reason why we'd had a rocky relationship for the past few years. This guy, though, probably just thought I was an unstable nutjob that routinely fell out with family.

In my drunken state, I stormed up to Donna and yelled at her, "Why haven't you told him what happened with Nigel?" I rarely lost my shit, but I could see the steam coming out of my own ears. It was like history repeating itself, where I had to pretend nothing had happened so that she could pretend that life was perfect.

Enraged that I had dragged this up again, Donna scowled at me and spat out one sentence that shattered my world. "I don't know what your problem is… it's not like he fucked you!"

And that was it. The relationship we had been trying to glue back together, patch over, and polish the cracks in, was instantaneously shattered. I stood there stunned, in the middle of the busy Spanish bar, watching her turn and walk away. Then I left the bar and walked back to the hotel in a daze.

My brother saw me leaving and followed me back. He kept asking what happened, so I told him. I wanted to leave. I wanted to get on a plane and never see her again. And that's what I did. My little brother used his credit card to book me a flight home from Spain, then I snuck out of the hotel in the early hours, making sure I avoided bumping into any of the other people in our party. I never spoke to Donna again.

My attempt at having a relationship with someone who wasn't capable of having a real and honest relationship with me was driving me crazy. Donna would never be ok with what happened because she couldn't face up to it; I would never be ok with it if I was trying to be ok with Donna. Surrogate-family or not, I had to cut her off.

For the next five years I had no contact with her at all. When I got a bit older and decided that life is too short to hold a grudge, I tried to re-connect. But to this day, nearly two decades later, she still refuses to talk about what happened.

I now have a choice. A choice about whether I cut her out of my life because I can't abide a fake relationship, or whether I decide to take her as she is – and probably always will be – and embrace some kind of a relationship with the woman that used to be my role model. A half-assed relationship, constrained to the conversational niceties we reserve for distant aunts and people you meet on trains.

I guess my choice will depend on how much I have left in my emotional reserve tank. And there are several other events that have taken a bigger priority on drawing from that reserve…

BREAKTHROUGH

CHAPTER LESSONS:

- Everyone has baggage. You just need to recognise when other people's refusal to deal with their baggage is stopping you from dealing with yours.
- Sometimes, closure arrives years later, long after you stopped searching for it, and it has NOTHING to do with others. Something inside you just shifts, like you've let go of a weight and you're back in balance.
- Occasionally, you need to lose someone in order to find yourself.

CHAPTER 4

Adam

Surviving the first year of university was a challenge in the aftermath of the Nigel incident, with me spending more time drinking than learning about law. Until I went home that Christmas, the only other person who I had told what happened was my housemate Becky. She was wonderfully supportive, but didn't know how to really help other than to assist me in polishing off a bottle of vodka.

On the days when I had a rare afternoon lecture, I would make the effort to drag myself in to the law school building as a distraction from my whirling dervish of a brain. It was on one of these afternoons, on a crisp and dry Monday afternoon, that I met Adam.

I was sat at the back of the lecture theatre on my own, avoiding eye contact with as many people as possible to try and hide my clearly red puffy eyes from the previous night's obligatory bedtime cry-myself-to-sleep routine.

The lecturer started talking and the hall of about 100 students fell quiet. He rambled on for a few minutes about something riveting to do with land law, and then the double door to the right of the lectern stage whipped open and in walked Adam. With a casual nod towards the lecturer, as if to say 'carry on', he sauntered towards the seat on the end of a row on the other side of the hall from me. And for reasons that I still struggle to articulate, he had my attention.

I spent the rest of the lecture glancing across the hall to sneak a peek and try to figure out why I'd never noticed him before in the (few) lectures that I'd attended. His cleanly shaven jawline flowed into a slightly dimpled chin, and his short, cropped hair was clearly trying to detract from an early receding hairline, so this guy wasn't exactly model material. But sitting at the back of the lecture theatre that day, I could feel his presence. I think it was because of his eyes – he had an intense, piercing gaze from behind his lightly-rimmed glasses, as though he was scanning his environment looking for prey.

The next thing I knew, people started to pack up their books and get up from their seats. Shit! The first lecture I'd been to in weeks and I hadn't listened to a single fucking thing that the lecturer had said. Oh well, it probably wouldn't have made much sense anyway! I shuffled out of my seat whilst watching this fascinating new stranger at the front of the hall get up and wander over to talk to a few girls sitting down the front. They all laughed at something and wandered out. *Oh, to laugh*, I thought, as I slowly made my way down the lecture room steps and back to halls.

As I arrived back in the four walls of my room, I dumped my bag on my desk and flopped on my bed.

I stared miserably up at the storage shelf above me, crammed with cuddly soft toys and pink feather boas that I had excitedly packed in anticipation for my new chapter at university.

The half empty pizza box that I had been too pissed and tired to dispose of in the kitchen the night before was still on my desk and had made the room stink. So, I swung my legs off the bed and went to open the window... and froze.

There, on the other side of the communal square outside my accommodation block, was the guy from the lecture, talking to the same group of girls from earlier. When they finished their conversation, he turned and walked into the building right opposite mine. *Oh, my God, has he actually lived there since I moved in? Why does it seem like I see him everywhere now? Is it like when you're a child and your parents get a red car, then all of a sudden you see red cars everywhere? Had he seen me before? Oh shit... maybe he'd seen me stumbling to the campus shop to buy more vodka, and in my half drunken state I'd never noticed him before?* Either way, my interest peaked as I resolved to find out more about this mysterious man. Maybe this was a good reason to start attending more lectures?

The end of the week came, and Becky and I did our standard Friday night out in the student pub that was on our halls of residence site. We sat at a round table for two, just in front of the bar – me with a double vodka and coke, and her with Passoa and orange juice. We'd discovered that her supporting my drinking habits by sharing my vodka wasn't in the best interests of her u-bend.

We were discussing her birthday activities from the week before when I looked up and saw those piercing eyes enter the room. I swiftly ducked my head and hid my line of sight behind Becky's face. "Shit, Bex, that's the guy I was telling you about from my lecture! Over there in the white top and glasses."

Becky whipped her head round indiscreetly. "What... the one with the receding hairline and massive forehead?" she mused.

"Stop it – he can't help it. Besides, he's so intense... I'm intrigued!" I replied defensively. "Anyway... I need another drink," I said slyly, as I downed what was left in my glass with a wink, as if to say 'watch this'.

I had previously been a courageous, independent, force of a young woman, and this quibbling, sorry-for-yourself wreck could fuck off. At least for one night. Although I was hurting inside, the vodka in my system had anaesthetised me enough to 'perform' on the outside. So, I puffed out my chest and strode towards the bar, sliding in beside my mystery man, throwing a coy little (fake) apologetic smile his way when lightly pushing in.

"Sorry... it's rammed in here, isn't it? You're in my law class, right? I saw you stumble in late the other day. Very cool. Looks like the lecturer really likes you!" I said with a confident swag, biting my lower lip gently and looking up from under my lashes.

When he looked at me, silent for a few seconds, staring at me with those piercing eyes, I felt like he had x-ray vision. Like he could see past my managed exterior façade and home in on the fearful little girl that was currently squished under a few layers of vodka. And I started to panic... *Oh God, what if he thinks I'm a pushy tart? What if he has a girlfriend? What if he realises I'm actually a fucking mess?*

And just as I was considering the best way to extract myself from the situation and retreat to my safe-zone, he smiled and reached out his hand.

"Yes... I am... I'm Adam. Nice to meet you."

I shook his hand, and so started one of the most destructive relationships of my life.

★ ★ ★

We spent the rest of the night in the pub, conjoining our two groups of friends, sharing stories about nights out and missed lectures, making plans to attend various events that revolved around happy hour and 2for1 deals on shots. Adam and I sat across the table from one another. I could feel his gaze on me, so of course I made extra effort to speak to the other guys in the group to pretend I was oblivious and not in the slightest bit interested. Then the last orders bell came, and we finished our drinks to start walking home.

The rest of the group walked towards their rooms on the south of the complex, whilst Becky, Adam, and I walked to ours on the north of the complex. By the time we made it to the communal square, I had already convinced Adam that he should come back to our flat for drinks.

As soon as we got up there, Becky responded to the tension in the air and loudly announced that she was tired and trooped off to bed, leaving me and Adam making small talk in the kitchen.

We took one of my many bottles of vodka and coke into my room, and he filled our glasses while I busied myself turning on my pink lava lamp, feeling like a proper temptress with ready-made mood lighting. I sat cross-legged on my bed while he sat in the chair at my desk with an uninterrupted view of my soft toy gallery, making me wish I'd been more of an adult when making my room my own!

We chatted shit about the world until 3am, veering from the intense to the inane with a moment's notice, and I was loving it. I laughed so hard I cried, and then I couldn't stop crying... *Fuck... stop it,* I thought to myself. *You'll scare him off with your emotional craziness!* But it was like, from nowhere, someone had turned on a tap and I couldn't find the handle to turn it off again!

His smile turned to worried concern as he realised the emotion behind my tears had switched from humour to sorrow, and I shook my head in apology as I retreated to my bathroom to mop up my tears and check that my makeup hadn't been completely fucked up.

A few minutes later I came out sniffing, and Adam handed me my drink and asked whether I wanted to talk about it. I replied that I was just dealing with some shit at that time, hoping that would fend him off, but in his true-to-form intense way, he held the silence, cocked his head slightly to the side, raised an eyebrow at me, and let his piercing eyes look through my soul.

And that was it... I couldn't keep it in. I blurted out everything that had happened with Nigel only a few weeks earlier, and felt an overwhelming sense of relief. Almost like that sensation you get when you've had to hold your breath underwater for so long you feel like you're going to burst, but then you get to the surface and gulp in as much fresh air as you can fit into your lungs. By the time I had finished, I felt like I had finally come up for air.

I looked at him for some kind of a reaction. I was DESPERATE for someone to give me a clue about whether this was a big deal or not. I was struggling, but Donna didn't seem to be. *Was I making a big deal out of nothing? Would this guy now think I was a drama queen? Would he think I was too emotionally damaged to have anything to do with?!?*

Adam stared at me for what felt like hours, presumably working through the verbal throw-up I'd just dumped on him. Then he got up from his chair and sat beside me on the bed.

"This is huge," he said eventually. "You've clearly been through a lot, and that's why nothing is going to happen tonight. We can talk about it if you want, or we can talk about something else. Whatever you want."

I don't think I've ever been so relieved for a guy to be in my room and say so categorically that nothing was going to happen. But right then, it was just what I needed. We chatted about various things for the rest of the night, and slept side by side, fully clothed, until about lunchtime the next day, when I woke to find Adam's arm around me. I'd never felt so safe.

Things with Adam and me did, of course, progress past the fully clothed spooning stage, and we went on to have a 'friends with benefits' kind of relationship. I joined his friendship group, would go to lectures with them and nights out, and when we were both pissed up, we would fall into bed, forming a routine that rested somewhere between a friendship and a familiar sexual comfort blanket.

He was a sounding board/venting outlet while I was trying to figure out how to handle my relationship with Donna, and a welcome distraction after I returned from spending Christmas at home having to face up to what had happened.

Things inevitably got complicated when either of us attempted to date someone else, as our boundaries and expectations were blurred to the point of being non-existent. But due to our individual relationship inadequacies, things with other people never tended to last long and we returned to our familiar comfort blanket. Looking back, I think it was easier for me to be with someone that knew all my shit but didn't expect anything of me than it was to try and start something 'proper' with someone new. So, that's how we continued for pretty much the whole of my first year of university. And things were fine – unexceptional, one might say – until my second year.

★ ★ ★

I came back from summer break to start my second year at university with a renewed sense of direction. I'd worked through some stuff in my head, and it was time for me and Becky to move out of halls and into our very own student flat. This was a fresh start, and I was determined to make the most of it!

This fresh start applied to me and Adam as well. We'd both decided to firm up our boundaries by attempting to actually have a proper relationship, and announced the big news to our friendship group. Expecting them to be as blown away by our big news as we were, instead we were met with rolling eyes and replies of "it's about time!".

So, we embraced "us" fully, and over the next month I ended up pretty much staying at Adam's house more often than I stayed at my flat, turning into one of those couples that seemed to morph into one person.

We ambled along peacefully until one night when we were walking back from the uni bar and saw a guy pull up in his car ahead of us, then walk into one of the houses.

Adam said, "Isn't that—?"

"Yes," I replied, cutting him off.

Adam had scowled at us several times in the uni bar when I'd briefly dated the guy the previous year. He had also been the source of a few tensioned silent spells, and I didn't want to repeat any of them. So, I quickly picked up the pace and turned the corner towards our house, talking to one of the girls in the group instead.

"Where's Adam gone?" someone in the group piped up.

We heard an almighty smash then Adam ran round the corner, ushering us out of the area as quickly as possible.

"What the fuck was that?" I asked, hearing some kind of an alarm in the background.

"Nothing," Adam replied, with an intense look of rage on his face. "Nothing he didn't deserve, anyway."

"What the fuck did you just do?" I asked, wide-eyed.

"He's just gonna need a new windscreen in the morning, that's all," he told me. "That'll teach him to mess with me."

I was, of course, enraged, and we argued for hours. But apparently it was my fault for "messing around with someone else that treated me like shit", and he couldn't help it because he felt so deeply for me. The one thing I will say about Adam was that he definitely had the potential to be a knockout lawyer, as he had a knack for presenting an argument that was so crazily compelling you actually ended up agreeing with him and apologising. And that's what ended up happening.

Rather than me think "what a crazily possessive knob-jockey!", I thought "Oh my God, I can't believe how much he cares for me." And instead of being concerned, I was sucked into a new level of attachment to Adam, with things becoming even more intense between us.

It got to the point where I was sleeping round there so much that I couldn't really sleep properly at my flat when I was on my own.

Adam was looking to become a Barrister after he graduated, and when Christmas came round, he decided to mark the occasion by inviting me to a Chambers ball that a friend of his family invited him and his housemate to. He made it very clear that this was a big deal so I had to be well behaved, not show him up in front of his potential employers, and if it wasn't too much to ask, it would be great if I could squeeze into a nice little dress.

Although not explicitly stated, it was clear that he meant I should attempt to lose a few pounds in the run up to the ball. And just in case the comment was lost on me, he would cook himself a bacon sarnie for breakfast and bring me up a banana, or order me a salad in the pub whilst he tucked into a burger. But again, rather than seeing this as a warning sign, I over-empathised with him, reminding myself that it was an important event, and it wasn't really that much for him to ask me to look nice. I told myself he took everything so seriously, he was really just looking after my health.

The night of the ball came, and we all left the house looking super glam and excited at the fun night ahead of us. We settled down for dinner, and I was on a table next to Adam, along with a bunch of random strangers that seemed pleasant enough.

I started making small talk in-between the courses, and by the time dessert came around and we polished off the cheese and biscuits, I was having a blast. Everyone was really friendly, and they were all really interested in talking to me, which was good because Adam kept nipping off to make brown-nosing small talk with senior-looking lawyers.

I polished off another few glasses of wine and went to find Adam outside, but he was nowhere to be seen. A few hours later, when it was time to go home, Adam returned to our group.

When we got back to the house, Adam was buzzing, having had a brilliant night. I was not, having spent the night pretty much on my own. When I received a message from Becky asking how the night had gone, I sat down to text a reply.

TEXT TO BECKY: *Eugh… he fucked off and left me for most of the night to talk to the Lawy—*

Adam snatched my phone off me. "Who are you texting at this hour?!" he said, reading my text to Becky. "Are you fucking kidding me?" he spat at me indignantly. "I took you to the ball and now you're acting like an ungrateful bitch. I thought you were having a good time?"

"Well I was, when you were there," I told him. "But it would have been nice if you'd spent a BIT of time with me after you finished your meal, rather than abandoning me with a group of strangers!"

And that was it. His intense face distorted in some kind of rage and he launched my phone at my head. Fortunately, I had sobered up enough to lunge to the side, so that it missed me by a couple of inches as it shattered on the wall behind me.

I can't remember what he said when he was yelling at me, but I was really afraid. He was livid, and lunged for me as I ran towards the bathroom, locking myself in. He was pounding on the door whilst I retreated as far as I could into the corner, curling up into the foetal position, hugging my legs up to my chest with tears streaming down my face. The pounding continued and just as the lock gave way, I heard his housemate's voice as he stepped between Adam and the bathroom door, asking what the fuck was going on.

The shouting slowly subsided, and after a few minutes his housemate came and coaxed me out of the bathroom towards the lounge. Adam was sitting on the sofa, hands tightly clasped and an intensity on his face that made a vein on his forehead so pronounced it looked like it was going to pop.

When his housemate retreated to bed, Adam began to speak very slowly and quietly.

"You know how much this event meant to me," he said, "I just wanted it to be perfect, and I HAD to mingle with the lawyers. And when I looked back at you, you seemed to be getting on just FINE with the guy sat next to you. So I stayed away, rather than us having an argument on what could have been a perfect night. But you've ruined that now, haven't you? I can't believe how selfish you are right now. Just go to bed and I'll see how I feel about this relationship in the morning."

I was reeling. *Had I been selfish? Was I flirting and didn't realise?* I guess I had had a few drinks… *Was this my fault?* I quietly made my way to the front door to go home, when Adam said, "Where do you think you're going? No – upstairs. Now."

And like the meek little lamb that I was becoming, I trundled upstairs and got into his bed. On the plus side, the fact that I'd shed a few pounds for the event meant that I didn't need any assistance in getting out of my dress, but my restless night's sleep was plagued with conflicting thoughts. I had been expecting an argument, but nothing like that. *How did I make him react so badly? Was he seriously thinking about dumping me?* That's not what I wanted at all.

In the morning, I woke to find Adam staring at me. "I've decided to forgive you for last night," he said, "just don't do it again. And don't you DARE flirt with people just to get a reaction out of me!"

In order to save my relationship, I nodded my head in acceptance and nothing more was mentioned of it.

When we weren't arguing, we were great together. We laughed, we talked, we spent a lot of time in bed, and life was good. The only time it was a bit awkward was when we were out in public together. If we were down the pub and a guy would talk to me, Adam would accuse me of flirting. When anyone complimented me on what I was wearing, Adam said I was dressing provocatively. And whenever we had a difference of opinion, Adam would ask if I was trying to wind him up, or – if it got really bad – test my reflexes whilst I dodged things flying towards my face when he lost his temper.

The next few months, although brief in the grand scale of things, turned out to be the longest few months of my life, and I can see now that I became someone I hardly recognised. I avoided eye contact with people I didn't know; I formed a bank of elaborate quick exit excuses so I wouldn't be left alone with guys to avoid Adam getting paranoid about anything happening; I became an expert at providing convincing backstories to explain his post-wall-punching broken knuckles to medical professionals; and I was walking on eggshells, taking his lead in conversations to avoid causing an argument.

It wasn't until I came home for a holiday and spoke to someone I worked with at a local café that I realised what I had become. I had asked for the weekend off, because Adam wanted me to go and visit him at his family home again, even though I was dreading it. It wasn't until my colleague said, "Are you sure you want the time off? Because it sounds like you're too scared to say you don't want to go, and that's not who you were before you went back to uni."

Her words hit me like a train. That was the wake-up

call I needed. It had taken someone relatively detached from me to comment on how different I had become from the person I had been six months previously. Just six months ago I could have sauntered up to almost anyone and brazenly pitched for what I wanted. Now, however, I spent so much time looking down at my feet I had a permanent crook in my neck, and apologised to people before even saying a word.

I immediately finished with Adam, and spent the next couple of weeks chastising myself for ruining his life – as he repeatedly told me when I broke it off. But then I managed to re-adjust to a normal perspective on life, and braced myself to survive the rest of my degree, hoping for a break from any more drama.

The funny thing is that once I ended the relationship with Adam, I never doubted my decision, and I never looked back. I had made my mind up, and I stubbornly stuck to it.

If I'm honest, I think that had I not still been reeling from what happened with Donna and Nigel, my relationship with Adam wouldn't have lasted five minutes. I would have seen him for what he was, rather than rationalising his behaviour out of a need for someone to accept and validate me. But without realising it at the time, my ability to leave him so easily… to compartmentalise… to put my thoughts about him in a box, and put that box in a vault… to have laser focus on the actions that would carry me away from him… had been honed from what happened with Donna and Nigel.

That shitty experience had significantly boosted my survival skills, and although I certainly can't say that I am glad it happened, I am grateful for what I could take from it to use later in life.

And unfortunately, those survival skills would be further tested in the not too distant future.

CHAPTER LESSONS:

- Some people are like infections – you're more susceptible to them when you have an open wound.
- When you don't recognise who you are when you look in the mirror, you need someone to hold up a picture of you from your past. If you're happy with the difference, live it. If you're not, unpick it.
- Things (and people!) that happen to you in life can cause scar tissue. But remember that scar tissue is stronger than normal tissue, and can give you the strength to do things you wouldn't have been strong enough to do otherwise. Don't seek out these scars, but remember that when they do happen, they can be embraced to be a blessing rather than a curse.

CHAPTER 5

Strike I

My time at university had been challenging, due to my struggles with Donna and Nigel in my first year, then Adam in my second. By the time I made it to my third year, I was a confusing mix of emotionally exhausted, anxious about what else life was going to throw at me, and apprehensively excited at the fact that this was all behind me and I could just about see the light at the end of the tunnel.

The previous couple of years hadn't been made any easier by the fact that within the first six months of my course I decided that I fucking hated law! However, my stubborn streak refused to quit, and the fact that I didn't have a bloody clue what else I would do meant that I had stuck it out.

I realised that whilst I was growing up, my career ideas had been largely driven by what I had seen on TV! In my younger years, I wanted to be a marine biologist because I loved the programme *SeaQuest* on TV, and had my first celebrity crush on the lead teenage boy living on the ship. Then I realised how much fish smell and that I don't like swimming in the sea, so swiftly moved on!

Then in my early teens, I watched a kids' movie about an ice-hockey team, so started ice-skating and fixed my sights on becoming a professional ice-hockey player. Then my mother paid for a few ice-hockey classes, and the reality of the sport resulted in me doing an aspirational U-turn quicker than you can say "Ow, that fucking hurt!"

Then I watched a number of programmes like *Law & Order* and *Ally McBeal* and decided that it would be really cool to say I was a lawyer... So that was that – I had made my lifelong career choice! I opted to take Law at A Level, found it quite interesting, and decided to apply to do it as a Degree.

HOWEVER... what nobody makes clear to you when you start considering degrees and potential career choices, is that most jobs have an underlying set of skills or attributes. If you possess these, you are likely to prosper; if you don't, you may struggle. And what was not made apparent to me until I started my law degree, is that an inane attention to detail is critical, along with a pathological need to find and win an argument.

I, on the other hand, had the kind of attention to detail that would see me book activity holidays for things that I had no idea about (turns out cross country skiing is NOT the same kind of thing as off-piste skiing!), and book hotels in one place and flights to another (Palma and La Palma are not only not the same place, but are not even on the same piece of land!). Coupled with the fact that I hated falling out with people and had an empathically debilitating capability of seeing credit in everyone's point during an argument, meant that I stood 0% chance of being a decent lawyer. This was only too apparent when I had my first assignment returned – I had basically used 1500 words to explain that both parties were in the wrong and should chalk it down to experience – with my tutor signposting me to the course transfer unit in the Students' Union.

But, as I said, I didn't have a clue what else I would do, and I was too stubborn to drop out, so I stuck at it, completed the exams, and scraped through to graduate. However, I did spend the last six months of my final year wondering about what the hell I WAS going to do as a career if I wasn't going to be a lawyer.

I spent a bit of time with the careers' advisors (better late than never!) and to this day I have no idea why this didn't jump out at me earlier! I thought back to all of the things that I had done over the years – the things that I enjoyed, the ones that I was good at, and those that I would say were my successes – and they were pretty much ALL around business, enterprise, and leadership.

As I mentioned before, at aged seven or eight, I would organise plays and dance routines for a 'show' when at my childminder's. Aged around nine and ten, I would save the empty After Eight wrappers in the box and use them as a mini-filing system for little Post-It notes on which I would write ideas for new businesses I could launch to make money from our neighbours. In secondary school, I would have a table at the fete to do face-paints, charging extra for 'custom' designs that strayed from the pictures I'd printed off the internet. And in sixth form, I was Chair of the Charity Group, organising events and services to raise funds.

At every stage of my life, I had unwittingly thrived in the world of business, so that's what I was going to do, I told myself in my latest career choice! I applied for dozens of graduate management consultancy schemes around the country… and got turned down from every one of them! My law degree appeared to be almost irrelevant, and I felt like I'd just wasted the last three years of my life. So, I downgraded my expectations and applied for assistant jobs closer to home, and went back to sticking my head in the sand by immersing myself in various 'drink the bar dry' end-of-year student events.

In the last week, Becky and I were returning from a meal out, before finishing off packing up the contents of our flat to move back home, when I received a phone call from one of the assistant jobs that I'd interviewed for a couple of weeks earlier. "We were really impressed with your interview, and we'd like you to start in two weeks' time," said the caller. "You've got the job."

I calmly thanked them and hung up. Then I squealed in delight and did a little jump for joy in the middle of the leisure complex car park. I got it! Someone actually wanted me! I felt like I'd just turned the page of a new chapter in my life. Ok, it was working for a small local company in my home town rather than a high-flying grad scheme in London, but it was a start. And I was sure that the starting salary of £14k would be negotiable when they saw how awesome I could be.

I told myself: I AM GONNA ASSIST THE SHIT OUT OF THIS JOB! Becky and I turned around and headed back into the leisure complex to celebrate in one of the bars.

* * *

It was my first day at work, on a warm and dry Monday in July, so I was up super-early to make sure that my make-up and hair were prefect. I had already spent what was left of my student loan cheque in Next to buy about four sharp suits. I would be the most overdressed Corporate Coordinator (AKA PA and general dogsbody) there was, but I didn't care. I had once heard someone say that you should dress for the job that you wanted, not the one you had. And as it would probably have been inappropriate to go in dressed as Wonder Woman, I figured this was the next best alternative. The power-suit look it was!

I drove in and nervously entered the reception area, and was shortly greeted by Mark, the MD who had interviewed me a few weeks earlier. He shook my hand (very!) firmly and greeted me with his strong, direct gaze, and booming voice. He was every inch what you would expect of a stereotypical male patriarchal leader, although his 1960s porn-star-esque handlebar moustache was a little distracting.

Mark showed me round the building and introduced me to the small team, whilst showing off some of their products. They were a small local company that had just landed a big contract with a multi-national fast food company to put public access internet terminals in their restaurants across the UK, hence the need for more admin assistance.

Everyone seemed really friendly, and I took a seat at my desk, sharing a room with the MD and the Operations Director. At the time, I was the only admin/co-ordination person, so it was clear that my role would be one without many boundaries, but that was fine because I liked variety. I liked being busy, and it would help me get to know how the business really worked.

So, I set off on my first task – putting together some marketing materials on their recent contract. My fingers typed so fast, they were making jokes about burning out the keyboard, but I was so excited to do something real and I was determined to do a good job of it. I printed it out and gave it to Mark to review. He raised his eyebrows and cocked his head, and I temporarily went into a state of panic. *Oh fuck, does he think it's shit? I mean seriously, what the fuck do I really know about marketing and press releases?* And then he broke the silence.

"Wow, this is really good. I wouldn't have thought to put it that way, but it really works. Well done. I knew someone with a law degree would be capable of this stuff."

So, it turns out that my law degree was useful, if for no other reason than looking good on my CV!

I was flying, as I smiled to myself and set off working my way down the list of other things Mark said he wanted done. I was so busy typing away that I didn't even notice that it had hit 5.30pm until Mark told me to go home. I packed up my stuff and left, feeling like I was floating on Cloud Nine.

The next couple of months passed in much the same way, with Mark throwing things at me to do and me relishing in the challenge to get them done. I would go to meetings and nod my head at things, and then run back to my desk to Google what they meant. When they asked for volunteers to do things like review policies or test systems, I threw my hand up and dived in. And when we hired a few more people, I helped with the interviews (like a proper professional!), all whilst also doing remedial tasks like picking up Mark's dry cleaning or smuggling him in a few Mars bars so his wife wouldn't realise he was breaking his diet. I felt like a proper grown-up member of the work team. Then suddenly, it was time for my three-month probation meeting.

Mark sat opposite me with a single, blank sheet of paper. He said that I'd done really well – handling everything that he and the team had asked me to do – so he would like to expand my role. They needed someone to help co-ordinate the installations for the big contract, and I seemed to be organised, so did I want to do it? I, of course, jumped at the chance – partly to work with a big named client, and partly because it gave me the excuse to raise my next point.

"I'd love to take up the opportunity," I said. "And as I have been here three months now, I'd also like to discuss a pay review. I think that the kind of things that I'm doing now, plus the extra responsibilities, would be in line with a £20k role." It was another thing I'd Googled. I was shaking on the inside, but tried so desperately to not let it show on the outside. Mark was the kind of person that considered himself to be like a lion – show any weakness and he would either turn his back to you or rip your head off.

"That's an awfully big raise from £14k only three months ago," he replied. "But you have proved yourself. How about we look at £15k?"

We were in the middle of a salary negotiation, and I was convinced my hands were shaking, so I sat on them and went in for one more pass. "I recognise my lack of experience, so maybe £18k would be fairer at this point in time?" Now he probably hated me and thought I was a cheeky bitch. P45 it might be then...

Mark smiled. "Ok. £16k final offer, with a review in six months' time."

"Done." I had the impression that my tenacity in raising my pay review and pushing him up on the amount had actually raised his respect for me. "And just one more thing," I said, as he raised his eyebrow. "I want business cards, so people know who I am when I meet them."

Mark laughed out loud. "YOU want business cards? Ok, consider it done."

The business cards arrived about two weeks later, just in time for my first meeting with the big new client. When Mark handed me the little box, anyone would have thought it was full of diamonds judging by the way my 21-year-old eyes lit up!

A couple of weeks later, I travelled to London with Mark and walked into the big client's Head Office in awe. It was HUMONGOUS, and full of professional people that knew exactly what they were doing. I felt like I was playing fancy dress grown-ups as we followed someone in a suit through to a meeting room and met with a load of people whose names I forgot as soon as I heard them. I sat in the meeting in silence, trying to keep up with what was being discussed. Something about tracking systems, an outsourced installation partner, and downtime tracking. I made a note of everything to go back and Google later.

Over the next six months, my confidence, business skills, and technical knowledge grew with an almost vertical learning curve. I developed tracking systems so we could keep a record of which computers were going into which stores (a glorified Excel spreadsheet!), I was the single point of first-line query for the engineers installing them in the restaurants (picking up the phone and putting them on hold while I asked the ops director what the fuck they meant!), and I learnt how to remotely dial into the store computers if they were reported as offline (which made me realise I needed to tell my brother to delete his browsing history more often!). All whilst still taking minutes, answering the phones, and picking up the MD's dry cleaning.

I felt like I had arrived in the world of being a professional businessperson. But this did also mean that I was staying later and later, often only going home at 8pm.

One day, we lost power in the office, so we all downed tools at 5pm and went home. I remember when I walked into the kitchen, my mother looked up at me in surprise and said, "Oh my God, did you get fired or something?"

I persevered, as I felt that what I was doing was being noticed and helping my career goals. As we were coming up to the time for the six-month review Mark had promised me at probation, I emailed him asking for the meeting but didn't get a response. He was a busy guy, so I waited a while and tried again. In the meantime, the contract had grown, and we were straining under the pressure. The sales guys were selling but the production unit wasn't big enough to keep up. The shipping and installation partners were less and less reliable as the volumes increased, and my manual systems weren't sophisticated enough to handle it. This meant that occasionally an engineer would turn up to a store and the package had gone to a different store, or the store hadn't been told and the guy couldn't get in.

I was doing the work of three people and starting to buckle under the pressure. Managing this project on top of doing things like sorting out the company insurance, processing expenses, taking minutes, organising meetings, co-ordinating events, and managing the HR stuff, was proving a bit much for me, but I hated to admit it. By this point, I had bounced back from previous life challenges by priding myself on my ability to cope with anything life threw at me, and work provided me with an undeniable thrill of achievement.

The long hours, though, had become a permanent fixture, and I would frequently cancel plans with friends in the evenings because I was simply too exhausted to manage conversation by the time I got home. I had started to feel like a bit of a machine, but didn't know how to change it.

When I finally managed to get my review meeting with Mark, three months later than planned, this is what came up. "Mark, you said we could review my salary at nine months, and it's now almost been 12. I've taken on so much more responsibility than is in my job description, so I think it's the right time to look to increase my salary. £20k is still the market average, so will you consider it now?" I slid across the table a number of job adverts and role profiles that I'd found off the internet broadly covering the same responsibilities that I'd accumulated.

Mark glanced down at them for all of three seconds before sliding them back across the table with a facial expression that distorted his handlebar moustache into a smirk. "All I'm seeing is things that are getting dropped, Sadie, so I don't see how you can justify a pay rise. Come back to me when you prove you're worth more."

His words stung, and I almost physically recoiled in shock as he got up and left the room. I went home and licked my wounds. Was he right? Was I bad at my job? I tried so hard, and had thought it was appreciated, but maybe it wasn't. But I didn't want to try any less hard. So, what was the answer?

I went back in the next day feeling apprehensive and rather deflated. I sat down at my desk that had piles of organised papers for the 98 million things that I had in play that week. Mark had clearly had a bad start to the day, as I could hear him shouting down the phone at someone from his office down the hall. We had moved into larger offices when we recruited more staff (another thing I had to organise), so I glanced up at the marketing girl sitting opposite me and rolled my eyes at her, just as Mark burst through the office door.

"What the fuck is going on, Sadie?" he bawled. "I've had the fucking installation engineers on the phone to ME, whingeing about the kit that's been shipped to the wrong depot. What the fuck is wrong with you? It's NOT THAT HARD!"

"I'm sorry, Mark, the engineer and the site confirmed everything with me yesterday, AND they called me on my mobile at 9pm last night to double check it. Look…" I rummaged through one of the paper files on my desk to find the electronically signed checklist.

Mark swept his arm across my desk, knocking all of the papers to the floor. "See… THIS is why you'll never get to where you want to be!" he yelled at me and stormed out, leaving me and the rest of the office in shocked silence.

I silently picked up the papers, and as the others slowly got up to help, I took myself off to the toilet, where I burst into tears. I felt like I had just had strips torn off me. Literally. It was almost as if something inside me had just shattered into a thousand pieces. I didn't know what to do with myself. I felt betrayed, as though all of my efforts had literally just been brushed off my desk in one dismissive gesture. I couldn't be there. So, I picked up my bag and I left, driving home through a blur of tears.

As I lay down on my sofa, my phone buzzed. I could see that it was the office, so I let it go to voicemail and waited to hear the message. It was Mark... furious that I had the audacity to leave without asking his permission first, and warning that I had better be prepared for a 'roasting' first thing tomorrow.

My sobbing came back with a renewed vigour. How could someone turn so significantly? I had thought I mattered, but now I felt like a commodity that was no longer in favour with the consumers. The thought of going in the next morning filled me with dread, so I did what every mature adult does... I got my mum to call in that I was ill, and I booked an appointment with the doctor for a sick note.

Sitting in front of the doctor, I sat down with a smile but started sobbing before he could even ask what I wanted to talk about. He asked me how many hours I was spending at work, how often I saw my friends, and how often I felt like I had fun and smiled. Thinking about it at that point, I realised it had actually been a while since I had been happy. I had put everything into my work and forgotten to look after myself. It was like I'd handed over the keys to my car and only just realised that I didn't like the way it was being driven, and that my fuel tank was empty.

The doctor said that he thought I had anxiety and mild depression, but that a lot of it seemed to be linked to the stress of my job. So he wrote me a four-week sick note and advised me to look at my options.

I went home and talked it through with my mum. She always knew what to do. When I told her what Mark was like to work with, she said, "Fuck him – he sounds like an asshole, and he doesn't deserve you. Let him find out the hard way how much you do there!"

So, I partially took her advice. I sent in my sick note – rather than my resignation, which my stubborn and fiery mother was advocating – deciding not to be rash and to see how I felt in a few weeks' time.

The irony is that a few days later I received a letter saying that Mark was very sorry but he was having to let me go… with no further pay. I opened the letter and felt like crying for all of three seconds, then realised that he'd done me a favour. Until that point, I had been undecided about whether I could go back to work for him, but the letter just made my mind up for me. No fucking way.

However, in this situation, not only was Mark an asshole, but he was also a misinformed asshole. Because although I didn't pay much attention at law school, I was pretty sure that if I was off sick and *I had handed in my notice* during that period (thus not actually working my notice), the employer didn't have to pay anything. *HOWEVER*, they DID have to pay you your full notice if you were off sick but *they fired you* during that period. And the latter was the case here. Despite the fact that I had been there just under one year, the contract didn't include anything less than the standard one month's notice (due to Mark not listening to my advice when I had pointed it out to him a couple of months earlier).

So, I did what any law graduate would do... I filed a claim with the Employment Tribunal and threatened to take him to court if I didn't get my notice pay. One week later, I received a cheque in the post.

It was good to know that my law degree had actually come in handy for more than just looking good on my CV... not that Mark would agree. I'm pretty sure that would be the first and last time he would be hiring a law graduate!

With the gift of hindsight, I can see that my first experience of work was a big lesson... one that I had missed. I put everything into the job, to the detriment of my health. At the time, I put my light brush with stress and depression down to the job that I was doing and what the working environment took out of me, but I never looked in the mirror at what I was doing to myself.

Nobody forced me to put so much in. Nobody told me to work all those hours. Nobody made out that the world would end if I didn't manage that contract perfectly. I told these things to myself. And it led me to my first strike in the cat and mouse game of stress and success.

I was about to move head-first into my second strike.

CHAPTER LESSONS:

- Some people are just assholes, and no amount of hard work will be enough for them. Don't let them build an empire using your blood, sweat, and tears as fertiliser.
- Pay attention in boring lectures... you never know when that little snippet of knowledge might make you thousands!

CHAPTER 6

A Twist of Fate

After my brush with Mark, I did some work for a friend who ran a few outside events and businesses doing a bit of everything, while I looked for another 'proper job' (and lazed around a bit over the summer months!).

Nothing really sparked my interest. I'd had my brush with office work and it didn't exactly inspire me to rush back to it, so I eked out the summer work – doing things like bar work at festivals and helping organise summer events. I was a few months off turning 22, and had gone from grasping my box of business cards like it was full of my life's hopes and dreams to bumming round in fields making minimum wage whilst dodging the British summer downpours. I was drifting after my dip on life's rollercoaster, and had no idea what I wanted to do next…

During this time, my grandma (on my dad's side) died after a short battle with stomach cancer. Dad was obviously devastated, and I remember thinking at the funeral that I had hardly ever seen my dad crying. The previous time was when he and Mum told me and my brother that they were splitting up.

I took a couple of days off my summer shifts to go

back to Cardiff with Dad for the funeral. It was the first one I remember going to as an adult, and even now I remember the ceremonial pomp – the funeral limos; the procession into the church; the march in front of the coffin; the hymns; the seemingly anonymous religious passages at the ceremony; and the obligatory throwing of earth onto the coffin... Even now I can remember how it felt so strange – foreign even.

To me, it seemed to be completely disconnected from the woman who was being buried. A woman who had fought her way through years of war, doing door-to-door sales to help put food on the table. A woman who had two sons, and then adopted a little girl in an age when adoption wasn't exactly the done thing. A woman who, despite her years, would tell me repeatedly when growing up that if sales taught her anything, it was that you always got more out of people if you smiled and got them to like you (often taking me out with her in the latter years, because it helped her sell more!), and never to marry a man until you had lived with him! She was anything but conventional, and very much prided herself on bucking the trend. Yet we found ourselves very much following the herd when marking the end of her life.

It was at that moment that I made a promise to myself: whatever I ended up doing, I didn't want a 'normal' life. I didn't want to be 'ordinary'. I wanted to be exceptional. To stand out. To do what others weren't willing to do. To stride ahead of my time, buck the trend, and beat a path for others.

I wanted to be like Grandma.

So, when my father told me a few weeks later that she had left me and my brother £5k each in her Will, I was faced with a decision. I had just been offered an administration job at a local Learning and Skills Council – a semi-public Government-quango managing funding for business training and development initiatives (YAWN!). It wasn't going to set the world on fire, but the pay was good, and it would enable me to use my £5k towards a deposit and buy my first house with my best friend. Or…

I could take that £5k and spend it on qualifying to be a diving instructor in Thailand! I had worked out that it would cover exactly the six-month course, accommodation, flights, spending money, and equipment. It was like it was meant to be… I'd researched it for weeks, and was online with it all queued up, my basket was full on the diving company's website, and I hovered over the 'Pay Now' icon…

So, having just made that earlier promise to myself of not living an ordinary life… I pussyed out, closed the browser, and emailed to accept the job offer. I took the public sector job and bought the house! *What a hypocrite*, I thought to myself. *But hey, I'll just make up for it with exceptional holidays.* So, I finished the summer working events, and at the start of September 2004, rather than slipping off the side of a diving boat into the Indian Ocean, I started my new job as a Contracts Co-ordinator.

I spent my first couple of months learning the ropes

– I was basically entering data from paperwork from training providers to pay them for qualification courses they were delivering using public funding. MIND. NUMBINGLY. BORING. And I was bashing myself for wimping out and taking the safe option. But there were a couple of unique public sector personalities dotted around the office that kept it entertaining, and the team were nice enough. So I settled in and started thinking about what I would spend my pay cheques on in readiness for Christmas and my new house, whilst at the same time cyber-stalking my former classmates to enviably watch them do things like travel the world and secure swanky suited-and-booted grad schemes in London. Fuck my life. I felt like I was compromising, and 'falling behind the pack'.

Then, on the 26th December, 2004, I awoke to the news that the deadliest tsunami in history had just hit the coast of Thailand. It was reported to have had the same force as 23,000 Hiroshima-type atomic bombs, left nearly 5,000 people dead, nearly 10,000 injured, and over 5,000 missing... and it had completely wiped out the island of Phuket where I would have been if I had made the alternative choice.

Had I chosen to go and be a diving instructor, I would have died. No doubt about it. I reeled in the gravity of the moment. It had literally been a 50:50 decision – I had been SOOOO close to going the other way, and if I had? Even to this day, that moment reminds me that all choices we make can lead us down fundamentally different life pathways – some good, and some bad. Some directly related to the choices we make, and some simple yet tragic twists in the fabric of life.

My decision to 'pussy out' saved my life.

CHAPTER LESSONS:

- I've said it before, and I'll say it again – sometimes not getting what you want can be the best thing for you.
- Don't compare where you are at in life with others. You will only ever focus on what they have and you don't, and we never look at those who are further back than we are. Looking at others to gauge our success will only ever leave us feeling inadequate, because we will always see someone 'further ahead'.

CHAPTER 7

Strike 2

Given my recent reality check, I made a New Year resolution – life is what you make it, and if you make a choice, make the most of it. So, rather than coasting, I threw myself into my public sector position. My job was data entry, but when the opportunity to do something different came up, I threw my hat in the ring.

Shortly after, they wanted someone to travel to Birmingham for three days to do some user testing on a new system they were trialling. My knowledge of systems extended as far as my remedial use of Excel when at my last job, so I definitely wasn't the natural choice, but I figured that if they wanted testers, then they should probably have the full spectrum of capabilities in there. And as no-one else wanted to travel away for three days, I was the only one that volunteered. I packed my bags and drove up to Birmingham.

It was the first time I had ever stayed away for work, and as I checked in and booked my table for dinner, I felt the familiar buzz of 'grown-up-ness' sweeping through me again. How glamorous to be staying away with work! I felt like I was back on track for success, and there was more in store where that came from…

75

Isn't it funny how things change? This was one of my defining thoughts in my early twenties (next to my business cards!), yet little did I know that this would also be the turning-point reason for me to 'semi-retire' from consulting in my mid-thirties. Living out of a suitcase is only glamorous when it's an exception rather than the rule, and you know you need to make changes when the Holiday Inn start sending you Christmas cards!

Anyway... the training was indeed mind-numbingly boring, but when I went back to work I realised that I could actually talk about what we should be doing with our processes with some air of confidence and authority. Then the conversation arose where they were talking about piloting their own bespoke system, and as I had done that training, I was asked if I'd like to help design the new system. I was no process expert and had only been in the job for about three months, while there were people who had worked there for far longer and were much more knowledgeable than me. But rather than shy away and hide behind my insecurities, I decided to embrace it as a stretch zone moment. I sat up straight, looked them in the eye, and said "yes, of course" in the most professional, faked confident voice I could manage. Then went home and Googled the shit out of database systems development.

I fluffed my way through the pilot system design, soaking up every word the developer said and regurgitating it back in the management meetings at which I suddenly had a seat. I very quickly recognised the importance of a good poker face – needing to constantly maintain a neutral I-know-what-I'm-doing-honestly face and tone of voice when questions and curveballs came up. I lost count of the number of times that a quizzical furrowed brow, accompanied with a tilted nodding head and assured mutterings of "hmmm... I'm sure that's covered, but let me just double check and come back to you", got me out of the shit when I didn't have a clue what was going on.

And it would appear that it worked, because when a promotion opportunity to become a Business Advisor on temporary secondment came up a few months later, they asked me to apply. Which, of course, went down like a sack of shit with the rest of the team, given that I had been there about six months versus their 10+ years! But I did the interview and nailed it (due to days' and days' worth of practice and research!) and was offered the position. I later discovered that many of my team had decided that I only got the job because I must have been sleeping with the boss (who was lovely, but NO!), so I lost what I had considered to be friends at the time. Compounded by the fact that many of the Business Advisor team, who were mostly grey-suited men in their fifties, didn't feel that my bubbly little blonde presence carried enough gravitas to be a Business Advisor, my first couple of weeks were challenging to say the least.

And deep down, I kinda agreed with them. I was supposed to be going out and about to visit businesses to advise them on how they could develop by doing things like training and Investors in People. But really, what the fuck did I know about running a business? I had a grand total of 18 months' work experience, and most of these guys (and the clients I was supposedly advising) had run businesses for longer than I had been alive. What the fuck could I bring to the table?

However, I persevered, and buddied up with a couple of the more approachable and open-minded colleagues, who showed me the ropes and helped build my confidence. I started helping run training sessions, which used some of the employment law knowledge I had gained during my disastrous degree years. And my experience of Mark growing a business without managing the people well or developing the infrastructure to help manage the growth, came in useful when advising some of the companies how they could avoid those same pitfalls. Maybe I wasn't as incompetent as I thought.

I became resolute in continuing to build my experience and confidence and make the most of the secondment opportunity – and to prove all of the early nay-sayers wrong! So, I took on more business sectors, travelled further afield, and threw my hat in the ring whenever the opportunity to do something new came up. Before I knew it, I had double the caseload and was struggling to keep up with the paperwork. People were chasing me for actions, I was taking work home, and I was breaking down in tears when my stupid crappy old work laptop kept crashing.

Yes, I had done it again. I had gone full-pelt, and run my engine down until it was empty. Strike 2.

But this time, I recognised it. I spoke to my line manager, who was incredibly supportive. She told me to go to the doctor, who signed me off for four weeks with stress, and I took it, sitting at home, twiddling my thumbs, 'winding down', not knowing what to do with myself.

When I returned to work, I had a meeting with her and her boss, and they were really encouraging, saying how valuable I was and how well I had done in the role so quickly. So, to help me maintain that performance, they were going to take one of the bigger business sectors off me to help alleviate the pressure.

WHAT! I felt like they had said they were removing one of my limbs. Did they think I couldn't cope? Of course, I could cope – I had just needed a break. How dare they? I wanted to move forwards not backwards. All of these emotions swirled around in my head whilst I politely nodded my head and maintained my practised poker face.

I went back to work feeling slightly wounded and a tiny bit undermined, but set my sights on getting back my reputation and exceeding the high-flyer expectations I was increasingly setting for myself. Now that I had more time spare than I was used to, I decided to fill it with other, more interesting things, such as helping one colleague deliver Investors in People training workshops.

I persevered for another couple of months, actually starting to enjoy the enforced variety of the role, when I was called into a meeting with my colleagues to be told that the service would be moving to another provider and some of us might not then have jobs. When my consultation meeting came around, it turned out that the Business Advisors would be transferring over, but because I was only on a temporary secondment contract, I didn't count as a 'proper' one. Therefore, I would be considered as still being a Contracts Co-ordinator so wouldn't be transferring. And as I only had 18 months' service, there would be no redundancy.

Are you kidding me? I've literally just bought a house! I wanted to scream. *I could've been a diving instructor by now (ignoring the little fact of the tsunami!), and you tell me this shit!* I went back to my desk a confusing mix of enraged and devastated.

I had really felt like I was on a pathway to somewhere. I didn't know where, but now it was literally being stripped out from underneath me. I carried on answering emails in-between trips to the loo to blow my sniffly nose.

Then I picked up a phone call which would change the course of my life forever.

CHAPTER LESSONS:

- Remember that we are creatures of habit. I had overloaded once, and blamed my asshole of a boss. Then I overloaded a second time, and blamed the fact that 'I just needed a break'. Don't be blinded by our often habitual urge to defend what we do and how we try to address the symptoms of our choices, rather than the root causes. I habitually overcommitted, and I needed to look at why, not chalk it down to "I just need a break".

- You will always have nay-sayers in your stratosphere. Some are up-front in their doubt of you, others hide behind positively framed sentiments like, "I'm just trying to look out for you." Use them as a critical friend – take their doubts and develop in those areas to prove them wrong. Say thank you, and wave goodbye as you see them disappear in your rear-view mirror.

- Seek stretch, and nobody can stop you. In the words of Susan Jeffers, feel the fear and do it anyway. Spot something that scares you at work, throw your hat in the ring to do it, and watch as it slowly starts to scare you less. If it doesn't scare you even a little, you're living in your comfort zone and not aiming high enough.

CHAPTER 8

Lift-off

The call was from one of the training providers that we worked with – just a routine check on what referrals we had lined up for them. But as I got on well with Jenny, I told her about the redundancies and that it had been a pleasure to work with her. She went silent for a few minutes, so I felt the obligatory British urge to fill the silence with a number of 'it's ok, I'll find something else' kind of assurances. Then she chipped in...

"How would you feel about working with us? It wouldn't be employed, mind – we need a self-employed contractor to go out to clients to conduct a business analysis and write a recommendations report on what they can do to improve the way they work. You would have to find the clients, but it's a free service to them because its fully-funded, so shouldn't be hard to 'sell'. And we would pay you £400 per client."

My jaw nearly hit the floor. My grandmother's advice had paid off well! I had always made sure that I had a friendly relationship with (most of!) the people I worked with, and it would appear that it really could lead to big things! My mind was whirring: going self-employed was a big deal as I had only just taken on a mortgage and there was no guarantee what I would earn; if I couldn't find the clients I wouldn't get paid; but £400 was A LOT of money for me, and I wouldn't need many clients to cover my bills... or to beat what I was currently earning!

My mind was split. Should I do what everyone else does and go and get another job? It would definitely be the safer option. I mean, what the hell did I know about running a business? Or... should I dive in and give it a go? I mean, what was the worst thing that could happen (gulp!)? And then my grandmother's words rang in my ears: "It's better to regret the things you have done than the things you haven't. So long as you learn from your mistakes."

My momentary hesitation ended as I responded, "Sure, why not?" I figured that if I fucked it up, I could just go and get a job! I decided that what mattered most to me was that I was brave and embraced opportunity, even if it scared the fuck out of me, rather than retreat into the arms of safety.

And so it began... I set my sights on my first business with all of 30 seconds' consideration and quick mental arithmetic that is even to this day renowned for dropping the occasional 0 and screwing up the numbers!

People still ask me today how I started out, and I'm always brutally honest – it was more through youthful naivety and a lack of a better offer than a headstrong determination and crystal-clear vision of the future. I didn't have a clue what was involved, how to set up a company, what I would have to do to keep it running, what I was going to offer, who would be my customers, or what I would charge.

Generally speaking, I didn't have a single fucking scooby what on earth I was getting myself into. So, I did what every self-respecting, first-time business owner does when they start out – I ignored the big, scary, important things and distracted myself by thinking of what I would call my company and sketching up a number of logo options!

During my four weeks' notice at work, I invested my time responsibly by booking myself appointments with 'clients' (that also happened to be my new accountant), sorting out my records (whilst making a note of potential clients and contacts for the future), and clearing my emails (notifying everyone of my leaving date and my new opportunistic availability as a freelancer)!

Every meeting I had made me feel like I was so far out of my depth I was in a different pool of water altogether. The accountant was talking about trading dates and tax liabilities; potential clients were asking for my fees and contractual arrangements; and former colleagues were asking where my website and cards were. I needed to sort my shit out and pedal a bit faster, because this self-employed train had left the station and was ramping up speed faster than I could learn how to drive it!

So, I called my boss, Julie, and told her of my decision to go freelance, and she was over the moon for me. She connected me with one of the business advisors she had previously worked with and who could access funding to help start-ups. The tables had now turned; I used to help start-ups, and now I was one myself! Now that I was in the eye of the storm, things seemed so much more complex than when I was independent and looking at other people's businesses. That objective perspective and clarity on priorities I had with everyone else's business seemed to have jumped out of the window when it came to my own! I needed help, so I called the guy Julie recommended and arranged a meeting in a few days' time.

The morning of the meeting I remember getting up extra early to rifle through my wardrobe and find the right thing to wear. My previous stock of power suits hadn't had much wear in my public sector job this last 18 months, so I went for the top-dog pinstripe suit to make sure this guy knew I meant business... even if, on the inside, I felt like a little girl playing dress-up.

I remember the guy's name even now. Andrew Parsons greeted me with such a warm smile and I instantly felt like I was meeting with someone who could easily have been my dad or something. Not one of these grey-suited pricks that looked upon me as an overambitious upstart (as I had expected!). I instantly liked him, and by the end of the meeting I left with the overwhelming feeling that he believed in my ability to do this business more than I did. And that third party, objective belief in me, where I didn't necessarily have it in myself, spurred me on to tackle the big scary things I didn't have a clue about. If Andrew believed I could do it (and he knew what he was doing!), then I had to give it a go and figure it out as I went along.

And that's what I did. I chose the name of my first ever company, designed my logo in a Word document, printed 200 home-made business cards myself, got a cheap two-page website made with the little bit of funding Andrew lined me up with, and filed the scary forms with Companies House and HMRC to incorporate the company. And that was me. A freelance consultant with my very own first company.

And I've been figuring it out – AKA making it up! – as I go along, ever since. I look back at that first company and can't help but laugh at myself. The business cards looked like they were made for a school project; the website was TERRIBLE (just as well nobody could find it!); and I had absolutely no standard pricing, paperwork, or terms and conditions. It's a bloody miracle that I managed to get any clients, let alone ones that would pay me for what I did. But I did, nonetheless.

So even now, when I am running my companies, I still ground myself in this experience, remembering that things don't have to be perfect – they just have to be good enough to work. I had to take myself out to market really quickly in order to make the most of the opportunities in front of me, but I wouldn't have made it if I didn't have that impetus, or had procrastinated over details and perfected my pitch first.

I have seen so many people fall by the wayside

because of this. So, just remember – you will NEVER feel ready. I didn't. Fuck, I still don't feel like I'm ready, or know what I'm doing *now*, and as I write this I'm on my sixth company…

My final day at work came and went. My ability to pay my mortgage at the end of the month was now dependent on me getting over my fear of failure. So, despite feeling like I was way out of my depth, I threw myself in… After all, you can't learn to swim until you get in the water!

My first Monday morning as a self-employed consultant, I had sorted out a desk in my bedroom, organised all of my stationary professionally as you would in a 'proper' office, and had my business cards sitting on my desk in front of me to remind me that I was now the proud owner of a proper business… But I was too afraid to pick up the phone! What if they didn't like me? What if they didn't want what I was 'selling'? Yes, I know it was free, but what if they hung up on me? What if they asked me a question I couldn't answer? All of my previous confidence seemingly still sat at my old desk in my old job.

As I played through a whole bunch of worst-case scenarios in my head and started to wonder what the fuck I had done, an email suddenly pinged into my new company inbox. It was Jenny:

Hi Sadie, good luck on your first day as a newly self-employed freelancer! Give me a call if you have any questions come up about the enrolment paperwork, and this is just to confirm that we can allocate you eight clients per month. If you don't engage with them all within the month, we can't roll over the funding, so go get em, tiger!

So, basically make sure you sign up EIGHT clients… don't let me down… tiger. The knot in my stomach tightened. Fuck, fuck, fuck… I HAVE to do this. Jenny is counting on me and she's taken a massive leap of faith in me to do this… I WILL NOT lose face. PICK UP THE FUCKING PHONE!

I took a deep breath and dialled my first company contact. I couldn't get past the receptionist – in other words, a polite fuck off. FAIL. Second call – got through to the small business owner but rambled on senselessly about what I could offer them, to be met with a polite but confused sounding "I don't think it's for us, but thanks anyway." FAIL. Third call – got through to the business owner's wife – fessed up to being new to this in the hope that she would take pity on me… and she did!!! Booked an appointment for me with her husband the next day. WINNER!!! I hung up and did a mini fist pump. Right – do more like that. And I did. And it worked. Within two days, I had filled up my eight consultancy spots.

I sat back and gave myself a mental pat on the back. I had just convinced eight professional people, who had run their companies for years, to invite me in to do an independent review of their strengths and weaknesses… and use my extensive 18 months' of work experience to tell them how they could do it better. What could possibly go wrong?!? It suddenly dawned on me that getting the appointments in the first place might not actually be the hardest part of this process...

I went home that Sunday – as I did most Sundays – to update my mum on my progress. She hadn't been hot about the idea of me going freelance, as she was acutely aware that I had just taken on a joint mortgage with my friend, and she didn't want to see me struggle, helpfully expressing her concern by sliding a small pile of job adverts across the table to me. "Are you sure this is the right thing for you to do, hunny?" she said, as she took a big sip of wine and a long hard drag on her cigarette. "These jobs are paying so well, and you'd be able to do them standing on your head. You wouldn't need to do cold calling or any of this tax stuff."

I love my mum dearly, and she would jump off a bridge if she thought it would help us, but she over-invested in me and my brother – most likely an after-effect of being robbed of raising her first two children. She dedicated 100% of her life to me and my brother, which I love her for, but it also meant that she struggled to take a more hands-off approach, letting us learn for ourselves, fearing for us to fail and suffer any pain ourselves. And at the end of the day, all she knew was her own path to date. She had never been self-employed, and although her dad had run a business, she had never been responsible for the health and happiness of her dad, like she was for us. Unfortunately, that concern was manifesting as a lack of support for my choice. Part of me was a little angry that she didn't seem to believe that

I could do it; the other part of me reminded myself that she was just worried for me. So, I reassured her as much as I could, whilst making a mental note to play down any self-doubt and fears I had when I saw her next.

Yet, however much I assured my mum, those feelings were still inside me – front and centre. I knew I had to push down the feelings of anxiety, uncertainty, and fear… *I chose to do this,* I told myself. *I will figure it out as I go along. This is my life now, and I will make it work. I WILL NOT FAIL.*

Little did I know that I was about to be introduced to a businessperson that would light up my life, and then later tear it back down again…

CHAPTER LESSONS:

- Sometimes, we are forced into decisions we probably should have made ourselves. I never would have thought I could go self-employed off my own back, but when I said that's what I was doing, my brother said, "I knew you would work for yourself someday." Which makes you wonder: if we saw ourselves as others see us (without our internal baggage and self-doubt), what would we do with our lives?

- Do the things that scare you. Even if you fuck it up, you're probably no worse off than if you didn't try in the first place. And even if you are, just make sure you can learn from it. My grandmother was a wise woman. It's better to regret the things you have done than the things you haven't.

- Sometimes the people who seem to not support your choices do so from a place of love and fear for you. Try to see things through their eyes and recognise that they're not trying to hold you back, but more likely trying to help you not to fail. They're not always the same thing, but they can come across the same way.

- You will never feel ready for something that you haven't done before. So, if you're starting a business for the first time, don't get hung up on perfecting your website, and marketing, and pitch, and business plan, etc; these things are important, but they're useless if you don't actually DO anything! Just get out there, cut your teeth by just doing SOMETHING, and consider it a pilot/opportunity to learn what does and doesn't work. I've learnt so much more by doing something, fucking it up, then learning from it, than I have from holding back until it's perfect enough to announce to the world. JUST START!

CHAPTER 9

Noah

I was starting to find my feet with how to engage with new clients, and quickly learnt that people are happy to help if you ask them for what you need. I was asking my clients (and friends) if they knew of other company owners who would benefit from a free objective review of their business, and the names came rolling in.

I had been self-employed for a couple of months when I decided that, although my degree was useful, I should probably look to study something more aligned with consulting and people management, which is the direction I seemed to be moving towards with the recommendations I was making and the consequential work I was picking up. People seemed to be accepting what I was saying, but I still felt like I was making it up as I went along. I decided to enrol on a part-time Master's in Strategic Management & HR at the local College. It's a fancy title, I know, but it's basically how to run a company and not fuck up your people in the process!

I loved what I was doing, but what I hadn't expected was that I'd be so lonely. That's the bit that nobody tells you about self-employment. You don't have the collegiality that comes with a workplace, and you don't have a peer or boss to bounce ideas off or get assurance from; it's all on you. So, I figured that maybe I could plug that gap with some of my course mates – a kind of study-based peer group.

I enrolled in August and started in September. Most people on the course were already working in HR or management roles, and looking to formalise their role with a qualification. I sat in the classroom and looked around. Everyone seemed experienced, and they were clearly batting at a higher level than me. I became acutely aware that I was essentially an opportunistic administrator with just over 18 months' real work experience who had spent that past few months bullshitting my way through small business consulting. Out of my depth yet again. *Just keep your mouth shut and look pensively intelligent*, I told myself, *and maybe they won't notice...*

The first few sessions passed, and everyone seemed nice enough. I had started sitting next to a woman who knew a few of the same people as me, and we got chatting about what I did. She seemed genuinely interested, so I asked the question, "Do you know anyone who runs a company that might want a free business development report?"

"Yes, I do actually," she told me. "You should speak to my friend, Noah. He runs a letting agency and a couple of other small businesses locally, and I'm sure he would be interested." She gave me his email address and I sent a quick intro message straight away, before I forgot or got distracted. We carried on with the course, and by the time of our next break, Noah had messaged me back and asked for a meeting the next day. *Another one in the bag*, I thought to myself as I drove home that night.

The next day, I decided to go low-key for the meeting, given that it was essentially a friend of a friend. I had arranged to meet Noah and his business partner in a bar just around the corner from me. I made sure I had my paperwork ready on the table: the funding form for signature, and the standard diagnostic template to make sure I probed into the right areas to diagnose what improvements could be made. Then I sat and waited, passing a few minutes by checking my emails on my phone.

Two pairs of feet appeared under my nose, so I looked up… and my heart skipped a beat. FUCK ME, HE'S FIT. I tried my best to maintain my professional poker face, but I think my surprise and delight must have been transparent, because Noah let out a nervous laugh as his crystal blue eyes met mine and he shook my hand, introducing himself and his business partner, Jim.

The intended 90-minute meeting turned into a three-hour courtship, crammed full of uninhibited story sharing, belly laughs that made your sides hurt, and a beautiful unspoken dance between overfamiliar, badly-veiled flirting, and a light touch attempt to remain a tiny bit professional and make sure I could make some vaguely insightful observations on my recommendations report.

We got to the end of the interview questions and our overt excuse for the meeting disappeared. It was clear that neither of us wanted to leave, but there was no legitimate reason to stay, so we said our goodbyes and I promised to get the report out to them within a week. I wanted to turn it round extra quickly so that I had a reason to meet him again to discuss the recommendations. It wasn't something I had done with any of my other clients, but he didn't know that!

I wrote the report the next day and got back in touch to arrange another meeting. Noah came back equally quickly to confirm – suggesting the following Friday at 3pm in the same bar.

It seemed like the longest week of my life, waiting for that second meeting with Noah. But Friday came around and I made an extra special effort with my hair and makeup that day, making the conscious decision to wear a slightly lower-cut top than I usually would for a business meeting.

Noah turned up alone. He said something about Jim sending his apologies as he had to be somewhere else, and I feigned mild disappointment and did my best to hide my inner joy at having him to myself for an hour. We dived into the report, and he met all of my recommendations with welcome ease and empathic self-deprecating humour that made me swoon even more. Before I knew it, we were done... after only 15 minutes!

My heart sank as he closed the report and thanked me for my hard work and quick turnaround. I stuttered as I started to reel off my standard thanks and goodbye patter, before he stopped me. "Now that we have work out of the way, you'll have to let me thank you with dinner and drinks. And we can start with the drinks now?" he said to me with a raised eyebrow and a gaze that clearly replicated my interest. So, this was it… now we would play the game of cat and mouse… overtly flirting with no business premise. It seemed he wanted to be as open about it as badly as I wanted to jump his bones. I replied with an equally raised eyebrow and a sassy, "Well, I guess it would be rude of me to turn you down, right?" Game on… business had turned into pleasure.

He returned from the bar with two large glasses of wine and a mischievous grin, and we proceeded to spend the next couple of hours talking about life, love, and the universe. It was like a conversational comfort blanket and felt like we had known each other for decades, as we shared stories of insecurity, inadequacy, and general fucked-up-ness. We weren't just on the same page… we were on the same letter of the same word. He shared my sentiment of feeling lonely in being a business owner, and feeling constantly like you're out of your depth and making it up as you go along. We both agreed it was great to meet someone else who just gets you…

We finished our drinks and went for dinner, where I was thrust into a table of about eight of his closest friends, including Jim and his lovely wife. And they all seemed to know who I was! It was interesting to watch how Noah was around his nearest and dearest, with no business veil to hide behind. He was enigmatic, extroverted, and socially inclusive as I watched him across the table from me from behind my fishbowl-sized wine glass, averting my gaze whenever he glanced across at me. I had spent a grand total of about six hours with this guy, and I could feel myself falling.

We proceeded to spend the next four days of our lives together as we entwined inseparably, sharing our hopes and dreams and aspirations for the future, including marriage, babies, and growing old. Over time, we went shopping, met the parents, and attended parties as if we had been a couple for two decades, not just two months. *This must be what people mean when they say that you JUST KNOW when you have found the one*, I thought to myself. I just knew, and it seemed like he did as well.

One day, we were in the car driving somewhere and he seemed distracted, glancing over at me with a slight tinge of anxiety in his usually lovelorn gaze. "What's up?" I asked quizzically. "Nothing, just thinking, that's all," he replied, taking my fingers between his and squeezing lightly.

That night, we were at a party, and again he seemed distracted. I noticed a dark-haired young woman staring at him intensely across the room, her gaze following him round like a lost puppy. "Who's that? I asked Jim. He looked at me awkwardly. "That's Joan... Noah was kinda seeing her before he met you. But it was complicated. She's just a bit intense."

"No shit," I replied, making a mental note to pick

it up in conversation with Noah the following day. We stayed for another couple of drinks then made our way home.

A couple of days passed, and I got the distinct impression that Noah was avoiding me. He wasn't responding to my messages particularly quickly, and was dodging my request to meet up for a coffee. Then he ran out of excuses and agreed to meet me. I wanted to know what was behind his turnaround over the past week, and I was determined to brave a difficult conversation if it meant we could get back to what we had.

As we sat down, he stared into his coffee, reluctant to look me in the eye – something he had been doing so intently for the past couple of months. He told me that he couldn't do this anymore… that he had some stuff going on… that I didn't know what I was getting into… and that it was best for both of us if we just ended it now. I, of course, protested, "It's fine, we can get through it." When I asked if he was still seeing Joan, he looked at me in surprise. "No, that's all over… but… it doesn't matter now anyway. Either way – we're done. I'm sorry."

And that was it. He got up and left. I was left reeling. How can you go from full-on to full stop so quickly? It didn't make any sense. I text him, pleading with him not to throw away what I thought was something special, but I had no reply. What the fuck just happened? I went home to lick my wounds.

A couple of weeks passed, and I bumped into several of his friends who were all as shocked and confused as I was. It still didn't make sense, but I hadn't had any reply to or even recognition of my messages, so I figured it was probably a definitive decision, despite my best efforts. Time passed and the hurt died down to a bearable yet annoyingly incessant low buzz in the background.

One night, I was out for a drink with Rachel, the woman who had introduced us, and couldn't help but have a whinge about men. My dating experiences since hadn't exactly made me grateful to be back on the market! But when I mentioned Noah, I realised she was avoiding my gaze and trying desperately to change the subject. "What's going on, Rachel?" I asked. She hesitated, seemingly weighing up the decision about whether she should tell me or not, then said, "He's had a baby... with Joan."

I went silent. The penny just dropped. That's why. That's why he couldn't be with me. The timing fitted. I'd met the right guy, but just a couple of months too late. Fuck. My previously building bitterness towards Noah subsided in an avalanche scale landslide. The intense stares at the party and the seemingly torn sentiment all made sense now. How could I resent him for trying to do the right thing? Perfect... now I had to get over someone I couldn't even hate. Great!

So, I did the only thing I knew how to do to take my mind off it... I threw myself into my business and filled the gaping "I think he's the one" hole with "I don't need men; work is a much more reliable investment of my time and effort" – a coping strategy that would go on to define who I became.

Little did I know that this wasn't the end for me and Noah, but the beginning of a set of circumstances that would go on to break me. Literally.

CHAPTER LESSONS:

- Sometimes, timing is everything.
- Sometimes, not getting what you want is a lucky near-miss. Even if you don't see it at the time.

CHAPTER 10

Imposter Syndrome

My strategy of throwing myself into work was working. I was getting busier and busier, and had less and less time to think about Noah. Many of the clients that I had done development reports for had come back to me and asked if I could help by actually doing some of the things that I had recommended (which they would actually pay me for!), like design a new appraisal system or run some management training. Of course, I said yes... then Googled exactly what was involved in doing so!

I didn't want to turn any work down, because I had become acutely aware that if/when the funding ran out for these business improvement reports, I would have to go out and find 'proper' clients that were actually willing to pay for my time. I couldn't face the thought of having to get a 'proper job' now; I liked the freedom and variety of what I was doing, and giving it up would feel like a massive failure. I HAD TO MAKE THIS WORK!

Despite my firm mental resolution, charging for my time was something that I was incredibly bad at. I would quote a set fee for doing a piece of work, like designing the appraisal system, and keep it low in case they might say no.

Then I'd spend days agonising over what should go in it, where the boxes should go, and whether a 1.25- or 3-point thickness of table lines would make it look more or less professional. I mean these were life or death decisions! I was still making everything up as I went along, because I had never even been around half of the things I was putting in place, let alone consulted at a specialist level with them. Most of the things I was creating had very firm origins in Google, or recently been mentioned on my course, so fell into my arsenal of "did you know?" conversations with clients the following week. Despite this, my clients seemed delighted with everything that I did, often saying that they had "just never thought about it that way before".

Nevertheless, I felt like a massive imposter and couldn't help but wonder why these people were listening to me. I would train small groups of managers and realise that they must know more than I did, because I'd never even been a manager! Quick, act like a seasoned professional and they might not find you out!

So, my poker face developed even further, and I learnt how to look like a seasoned pro on the outside, whilst containing the scared little girl on the inside. I overcompensated with an assertive presence, and frequently found myself taking a Superwoman-styled, hands-on-hips power pose on the outside whenever I felt a little shaky or insecure on the inside (which was often!). In fact, I did it so often that it went beyond a habit. I think I actually managed to convince myself that this was the real me.

I was a self-assured, confident, courageous young freelance consultant, and I could handle ANYTHING! Fear? BE GONE! Insecurity? DO ONE! Self-doubt? FUCK RIGHT OFF!!! I was living in my stretch zone, and I got so used to it that my comfort zone became boring. I was hungry for new experiences, and my lethal cocktail of lofty self-expectations, high effort, and an absolute refusal to fail, meant that I was throwing my hat in the ring for bigger and bigger work projects to just see how I could cope. I had become addicted to achievement, and my tolerance levels were rising.

A few months into my Master's course, we had studied a few strategic business models and I was blown away. *OMG, this is the kind of thing that I have been doing in my head (making up as I went along) and there's an actual professional model behind it,* I thought. I felt validated and inspired at the same time. This is what I wanted to be focusing on – what makes a business tick, where it wants to go, and how to bridge that gap. I decided in that instant to raise my game with my clients, and to focus more on the strategic level 'stuff' rather than 'fannying around with basic stuff' like appraisals and day-to-day challenges. And I needed to find a better financial model, because charging by the hour was fine but it was a lot of work for not much money (my financial expectations had risen rather sharply!). The work was consistent, but I rarely had more than a handful of hours' work each day. I made a note to myself: be on the look out for related, but better, opportunities. Very specific, I know!

Then, almost as if by magic, a couple of weeks later I received a call from one of my former colleagues saying that since the transfer to the new organisation their agenda had changed a bit, and rather than just doing 1:1 advice, they wanted to offer large room training events for business owners. There would be about 50 people per workshop for a full day's training, and they needed to use an external contractor to deliver the training. Was I interested?

I gulped... 50 people? The most I had ever trained at any one time was four or five, and that was on something that I had designed. What the fuck could I train a room full of experienced managers on? And then they explained that it would be taking these people through a few management models, like strategic planning, etc, and did I know any? Bingo! I dazzled them with my new-found understanding of strategic management models as if I had been practising them for years, and my authoritative tone and use of lots of long words to mask the bullshit I was making up was so impressive that I almost believed it myself! That was it – the gig was mine. I put down the phone and noted to myself how it's funny that things can fall in your lap when you're in the market for something new.

* * *

The first workshop came around quickly. As I stood at the back of the room watching the seats fill up with small business owners looking for help and guidance, I found myself doing the Superwoman pose. *I'VE GOT THIS. I'VE GOT THIS*, I kept repeating to myself, hoping that I might actually believe it and stop my hands from shaking with the adrenalin and nerves coursing through my veins.

A number of my former colleagues were at the event to meet their clients and to do some networking, so I was also very conscious that the stakes were high. I couldn't fuck it up because the nay-sayers would see. *I WILL NOT BE OUTED! Not today, anyway*, I thought, as I fiddled with the name lanyard that they had given me to indicate that I was part of the organising team.

I was deep in thought about how I would open up the event when a grey-suited man with an equally grey flop-top of hair walked up to me and said, "Tea, white, with one sugar, please."

I snapped out of my internalising. "Sorry?" I said, confused.

He pointed to the teacups on the table next to me and raised his eyebrows at me. "Tea, with milk and one sugar," he repeated with a light dusting of condescendence. Oh, he thought I was the refreshments girl. I didn't quite know how to react, so I reached for a cup and prepared his drink. "Good girl," he retorted with a dismissive nod of his head, before walking away to find a seat.

My head felt schizophrenic, battling with two extreme reactions at the same time. On one shoulder, the indignant, defiant, and self-assured side of me was raging. *HOW FUCKING DARE HE! Who does he think he is? The sexist, misogynistic pig. I'll show him!!!* Whilst on my other shoulder, my inner little girl popped her head up. *OMG, he saw me. He saw ME! Me for what I really am. I shouldn't be here doing this – what the fuck do I know?!?*

I felt the anxiety rise to a level of panic and I wanted to bolt. I wanted to run away from this room, from this audience, and find a safe space to hide until it was over. But then my mindset stepped back in, and metamorphosised into a full-blown metaphorical suit of armour. It was like the pressure on my emotional boiler rose to dangerous levels and the override switch just kicked in to stamp it all back down again. I had pressed a button and an Iron Man-style suit of armour was clunking into place around me. *YOU WILL NOT LOSE FACE. YOU WILL NOT FAIL. YOU'VE GOT THIS...*

I took a big breath and walked to the front of the room. I stood so tall and straight it was like I had a rod up my backside. The room fell to a hushed silence. "Good morning, everyone... my name is Sadie and I will be your trainer today." My eyes met with the grey flop-top man, and he nearly spat out his tea.

I set the tables off with a short introductions exercise, then hushed them to take some feedback and see exactly what they wanted to get out of the session. I heard from a few people, and then we got around to flop-top man. Fabulous. Let's dance, Mister...

"So, what specifically brings you here today, and what would you like to get out of the session?" I asked with as much of a professionally neutral tone as I could muster.

He puffed out his chest, opened his mouth, and spoke with as much humility and grace as Donald Trump. "I run a training company, and I'm just here to network and meet new people that I can help."

I pasted a wide but tightly-lipped smile on my face. Right, so he'd come to MY training session as a way of trying to sell to MY delegates? *I don't think so, Mister.* My suit of armour was charged and locked onto its target.

"Well, I'm sure there are some things that we can do to help you improve your business as well," I responded with an assertively feigned helpfulness that failed to mask the "fuck you" sentiment underneath my words.

The room took a coordinated, audible sharp intake of breath, and I had a momentary flash of panic. *Fuck, do they hate me? Did I do the right thing to call him out? Is he gonna hit back?!?* But rather than show any of these internalised doubts on my face, my poker-faced suit of armour disengaged, as if to say, "I'm done with you now, little man." Then I turned to the next table, and with a beaming smile said, "And what were some of the key objectives that came out of your table's discussions?" Without skipping a beat, we were back in the moment and ploughing on with the agenda.

The rest of the morning went by in a blur, but at lunchtime a number of the delegates came up to me and said "well handled" with a knowing wink.

I had taken a courageous gamble, and it seemed to

have paid off. Feel the fear and do it anyway! I had the room eating out of my hand, so I made a mental note to remember that sometimes you have to ignore the voices in your head. If you project confidence, people tend to respond confidently. So, I added this to my arsenal; my armour just got an upgrade. Not being confident was now not an option. This was Sadie 2.0.

On the outside, Sadie 2.0 was stretching, extending, and growing. On the inside, however, the foundations were starting to creak. The scared little girl had been resigned to a small corner of my being – out of sight and out of mind, but not out of place.

CHAPTER LESSONS:

- Working for free (initially!) can actually lead to genuinely valuable (and financially rewarding!) client work – you just need to know when and how to move from one to the other by managing their expectations clearly. Had I not done some free work with most of my clients initially, they wouldn't have gotten to know (and hopefully like!) me, or built up any confidence that I could add value. That then helped me to justify my fees when the funding ran out.

- When I started securing clients, I still believe that they chose to work with me because they LIKED me! I was by no means the most specialist consultant out there, but the fact that I was approachable and likeable meant that they chose me over other more established people. So, never underestimate the value that YOU bring to your work as a human being – your knowledge and skills will only get you so far. And you can't get people to like YOU if you hide YOU behind a wall of professional bollocks. Learn how to bring yourself into your work and you will begin to stand out from the crowd.

- When starting out, we rarely feel like we are worth our fees. But instead of thinking 'what am I worth?' focus on 'what is this worth to my client?'. The people you work with usually struggle to find the time, focus, and objectivity to do half the things you might be doing, so even if it doesn't seem like rocket science to you, they are being given something they wouldn't otherwise have access to without you.

- The fact that I wasn't experienced in half of the things I was consulting on was actually a strength. It meant that I had a level of open-minded, unassuming objectivity that allowed me to look at things differently and to come up with ideas that weren't 'established thinking'. So, remember that the things you are NOT can also be a strength when leveraged correctly.

- Step towards the things that scare you and you will move forward so much quicker than if you step back from them.

Nothing Ventured, Nothing Gained

I had been in business for about 18 months, and it was growing. The funding had stopped, but the clients that I had already picked up were asking me to do more and more things for them, and they were referring me to other business owners they knew.

As a result of running the large group training sessions and realising that I could do training – and that I actually quite enjoyed it – I had put on a few open sessions myself, and been delighted to see a fair number of businesses turn up. *OK, this is another arm to my business,* I thought to myself. *What can I do to make it bigger, better, and more frequent? Stretch before you get used to standing still!* Being paid for a full day's training seemed like a much better financial model than hourly consultancy services, so I steamed ahead to try and realign my business.

I updated my CV with all of the training topics I thought I could cobble together (from Google) and emailed it out to a load of training companies, including local colleges and national awarding bodies like CMI and CIPD (the main awarding bodies for chartered management and HR qualifications).

In a funny twist of circumstances, the college where I did my Master's 1st year (I had moved over to Oxford Brookes to do the second and third years in a one-year condensed course) asked if I could come in and teach the HR qualification that they ran. So, I ended up training a room full of HR professionals before I had actually finished my own qualification!

One of the many emails I sent out seeking training work brought a response from a man who agreed to meet with me to discuss what I could do. However, when I met with the guy, he basically used the meeting as an opportunity to spell out why I didn't have the experience or gravitas (AKA I wasn't old enough) to deliver his programmes, and I left with my tail between my legs. My inner little girl completely agreed with him, but I figured 'nothing ventured, nothing gained' and picked myself back up off the floor to try again with someone else.

A few days later, I received an email from another training company. They were interested in my management and HR skillset, because they mainly did IT training but needed a 'specialist' for the people-related training their clients required. I re-read the email several times, beaming at their use of the word 'specialist'. Did I count as a specialist yet? Maybe not, but if that's what they wanted to believe, then who was I to disagree? I arranged a meeting with them, at which

I delivered a 30 minute-tester training session to show them my style. I was absolutely shitting a brick when delivering it, as I was presenting to three women who all had training backgrounds, but I must have pulled it off sufficiently as they offered me a freelance contract and my first booking there and then.

And that was it. Within one week, I'd gone from having strips torn off me by one guy who told me in no uncertain terms that I was too young and inexperienced to deliver training to business audiences, to being signed up as a specialist by another company. My head was reeling – I didn't know whose opinion to believe. Had I just been lucky and duped these nice women into signing me up? Or was that guy just a prick who liked putting people in their place? I didn't know. But the training day rate was attractive enough to make me push past my self-doubt, so I decided to trust the ladies' judgement and chalk the experience down to that guy just being a dick!

The next six months just flew by, with me taking on more and more training, often staying away from home three or four nights a week. I could be travelling from London one day, then up to Scotland another. My ego was flattered by the demand for my skills, and living out of a suitcase was workable while I was in my mid-twenties. I enjoyed the variety, sharing stories with my friends and family about where I had been and things I had seen.

When delivering the training, I was always insecure about not knowing enough about the subject I was going to be presenting, and would spend hours researching the topics, staying up late at night to prepare handouts and flipcharts so that my delivery would appear to be seamless. And it seemed to work. The feedback was always good, and as I kept getting booked, I decided that I should maybe park my insecurities and actually start to trust in the evidence amassing around me. My head agreed... but my heart (and the little girl sat next to it) remained unconvinced.

At one networking event, I had bumped into a guy who also ran a small training company with a couple of offices. They were looking for associates, and we got on well, so I agreed to go and have a look at their offices and meet his two partners. I went in about a week later and really liked what I saw, so agreed to do some training for them. But these guys needed training actually designed against client needs (whereas I had previously just been delivering already designed courses). This would require me to attend client meetings with the directors to help understand what training they needed, then go off and design and deliver something to fix it.

I realised that the path I had taken was finally merging all of my previous skill sets: the business diagnostics I did when I first started out helped me to understand their business and identify what their challenges were; my small business consulting helped me bond with the client and recommend what could fix their problem; the pre-designed training courses I had been delivering gave me a good understanding of what kind of content might go into a training course; and my HR training helped me to identify the people practicalities behind the theory. All of a sudden, I realised that I had a foot in training and a foot in consultancy, each of which brought the other alive in a practical way. Rather than just training in theory, I could use my (somewhat limited!) consultancy experience to bring the content to life, and rather than just consulting to advise people what they should do, I could actually help them develop the skills to do it themselves. *Hmmm…* I thought to myself, *funny how all those things I did when I just thought I was chasing the next piece of work have come together to give me a differentiator.*

I carried on providing more and more training, only occasionally carrying out a piece of consultancy work for one of my old small business clients if they specifically asked for help. I was delivering training 2-3 days a week around the country, then coming back to Swindon to deliver the HR qualification at the local college one day a week.

My earnings were consistently high enough to live well, and as I had almost three years' trading history by this point, I decided to take the leap and buy my own house. I found somewhere I liked, sold my half of our house to my friend, and moved into my very own two-up, two-down, end-of-terrace house. I was proud as punch and was busily filling it with colour-co-ordinated accessories, when the recession hit six months later. FUCK!

I knew that many of my clients would be tightening

their belts, and I would need to do something to make sure I didn't lose my house if my work dipped below a certain level. I was mulling over my options and talking through my thought processes during a meeting with Phil from the partnership, when he made me an offer.

"Well, it seems silly us both trying to fight our way through to clients' doors in hard times – why don't we join forces and do things together? We're using you consistently to deliver training, but we also need help developing our business, so why not come and work with us more closely?" He paused with a hopeful inflection in his voice.

I wasn't sure what to say, but committed to thinking it over and coming back to them. The logical part of me knew it made sense. Merging the work from both of our businesses would mean I would have a regular salary to average out the financial ups and downs of working on my own, whilst still keeping the kind of flexibility and variety that I was used to. But a little part of me bucked at the thought of 'going back' to a salary instead of my freelance model. *Was this a failure? Was I selling out?* I wondered. *Was it a temporary stopgap, or the start of the end where I would never go back to being self-employed again?*

I was uneasy, but knew that it was the sensible option. And I did know these guys, I knew what I would be doing, who I would be working with, and could pretty much set my own terms. If I was being honest, the only thing holding me back from saying yes was my ego. I decided to bite the bullet and joined them in a flexible role that bridged a whole number of things, from HR Director and Strategic Partner, to Business Development and Training Consultant.

And I loved it. I'd forgotten how much I missed having colleagues. Even though I was still travelling away a lot, it was nice to have someone familiar on the end of the phone to have a whinge at when things happened, or someone to bounce ideas around with. And we all got on really well.

We had been working together for about a year when, chewing the fat at a directors' meeting one day, one of the team mentioned a conversation with an awarding body for whom we delivered management qualifications. The discussion had centred around their growing use of e-learning and the hassle of marking and tracking assignments for qualifications. As we were all ideas people, we began discussing some suggestions until someone said, "Why don't we design our own system that will use e-learning to deliver these management qualifications, as well as automate the assessment process?"

My eyes lit up. A NEW PROJECT! I love a good project! I was like a magpie with shiny things when it came to new projects start-ups, and I wanted in! We bandied a few ideas around, and then all eyes fell on me. "Would you be interested in coming in as a partner with us, Sadie?" I was asked. "You'd be much better at managing its design and launch than we would be, as we have to manage the training business as well."

I was flattered. These guys, who had been in business for over ten years, wanted to go into business with me! My inner little girl blushed coyly, whilst the outer-armoured me replied in a confident, assertive tone, "Yes, of course." I was sure I could Google whatever was involved in designing e-learning and a system. *It couldn't be that hard, right?* I thought. *After all, nothing ventured, nothing gained! What's the worst that could happen?*

I had just taken a huge leap 'up' in the business world. I was about to launch my second company (but this time with business partners!), and my head was full of the possibilities of this new opportunity… certainly not the near bankruptcy and breakdown that ensued…

CHAPTER LESSONS:

- You will meet lots of people – some will help pull you up, others will try to hold you down. You get to decide which ones impact the way you see yourself. Sometimes, people's judgement of you is more about them than it is about you.
- You can use your inner critic and insecurities to make you better – focus on what they say and work on the things you can do something about, and chalk the things you can't do anything about down to a "what's the worst that can happen?" shrug your shoulders moment. That way, your inner critic becomes your critical friend.

- I learnt not to trust my insecurities. Instead, wait to see what actually happens, and park your insecurities if they don't match the results you deliver.
- Sometimes your disparately different areas of experience can align to mean that you are in the perfect position to make the most of an opportunity, so NEVER see something you have done in the past as a waste of time. I would never have had the opportunity to start this new venture without having done the systems work in my first ever administration job straight from uni.

CHAPTER 12

A Bridge Too Far

We had launched the new company and agreed a name. But this time, we had engaged a digital design company to build us a website and brand, so it already looked a shit-lot better than my initial attempt at my first company. We had also canvassed a few firms that could design the system for me. Everything they said seemed like a foreign language – LMS, SCORM compliant, UEX – all of course noted down and Googled later on. But this time I had to know more than just the language. The success of this venture was 100% down to me, and now I had business partners who were reliant on me to deliver. The stakes had risen, and I was locked in for the ride!

We decided to use an Indian company to design the system for us, and naturally they needed a retainer to start work. We managed to access some innovation funding to help with some of the costs, but we needed more. Phil had some money set aside, but as a shareholder I needed to contribute as well. Of course, I had been sensible with my money and spent it all on colour-co-ordinated accessories in my new house. So, I had a decision to make: if I was going to make this work and be an equal partner, I had to take out a loan. I had done that before, but never for business purposes. Weirdly enough, the risk seemed higher when considering a loan for business purposes which should (hopefully) ultimately be able to be paid back, than it did for spending on something like a car, which would only ever cost you money.

I thought long and hard, and spoke to my parents. My dad, ever the safe bet, wasn't keen for obvious reasons. My mum, true to form, said, "You've gotta be in it to win it," and to go ahead. That meant the decision was all on me. If I borrowed the money and it didn't work out, I would have to pay it back out of my own pocket. So, I needed to put in only what I could afford to lose. £15k seemed to be an acceptable amount, as I felt the repayments wouldn't exactly bankrupt me if taken out over a five-year period and it didn't work out. Taking a big gulp and crossing my fingers and toes, hoping for the best, I dived in and took out the loan.

We commissioned the Indian company to start the design, and a couple of weeks later I was on a plane out to India to help test and refine the system. In a stroke of luck, I wangled a free upgrade, so was snug as a bug in a rug in my Business Class, lie-flat British Airways bed, thinking to myself that this was what it was all about. My chauffeur-driven car picked me up from the airport and took me to the hotel, and each day the team showed me what they had done as I picked my way through it.

Again, I wasn't exactly a systems expert, but I'd

realised that I had managed to figure most things out over the past few years, and if something didn't make sense to me when I dug a bit deeper, it was probably because something wasn't right. So, I asked lots of questions, and we tried to figure everything out despite our awkward half-English, half-gestured exchanges. I was surprised that I found myself using a lot of the insights I had gained when working on the system design project in my first job after uni. I still felt like I was making it up as I went along, but maybe my knowledge wasn't as limited as I'd initially thought.

I returned from my first trip to India and ramped things up. For the training business, I was still attending client meetings, securing new business, designing and delivering training, developing the business cashflow, and handling the company's HR issues across its three offices. On top of writing the content for the e-learning modules, I was testing the system changes, reviewing and editing the e-learning modules they had coded, writing user guides, organising pilot demos with potential new clients, and organising the system launch at a forthcoming big conference. I was also staying away from home almost five days a week to deliver training or travel between the three offices, communicating with India outside of office hours to accommodate the time zone difference, and making return review trips every 2-3 months.

My propensity to convince myself that I could handle everything had led to me spinning way too many plates, and the new company had been a bridge too far. This, on top of the fact that I was making the loan repayments, had meant that I was under increasing financial strain and mounting emotional pressure to make it all work. Added to that, the main training business was starting to struggle in the aftermath of the recession and, of course, I took it upon myself to try to fix it.

"We need to restructure the business," I said bluntly to the other partners in a management meeting one day. "We have staff attached to declining services, the funding work we do is reducing, and we need to up our game to compete in a tighter market. And we don't need three offices. If you want your business to continue, you need to make some difficult decisions." I had never been one for sugar-coating things…

I was met with a tirade of "you don't understand" and "we've built this business from scratch" and "but people are counting on us". The partners were basically unwilling to make any substantial changes. Apparently, "we just need to make more sales" was their view. As if it were that easy!

I left the meeting with a sense of unease, which wasn't made any better when Phil came to me later to discuss putting more money into the design of the system to enable additional features. I was reluctant, saying that I thought we should sell it first and then develop it with the money it made and the client feedback gathered. Plus, I couldn't leverage any more money, so Phil said he would put more of his cash in and just take it back out as a loan when the system started making money. *Ok*, I thought, *if that's what you're happy with*. But my unease was growing.

As a partnership team, we seemed to be growing apart; we had fundamentally different ideas about how we should be managing the businesses. Although I wasn't a shareholder in the training business, by this point I was very much responsible for making it a success. But they were not willing to consider what I believed was necessary to achieve that. And I was starting to wonder whether the e-learning system was just a bridge too far for me/us/them. Maybe I had made a mistake getting involved?

My head was whirring on a daily basis, and I felt increasingly trapped in a business that I was responsible for but had no power to make work. Had I gone too far down this road to turn back?

I was out one night having a (rare) drink with friends and listening to their general woes, when I realised that I felt so distant from the everyday that I struggled to relate to them. I was approaching 30, and hadn't had a date for just over a year. I rarely went out socially, and had become a very boring person – all I could talk about was work, and even that was pretty shite!

I wanted my life back, but had no idea where to start. I HAD to make some changes, but had no idea what I wanted. I couldn't change the work stuff, so I decided to look elsewhere to make changes.

In the corner of the bar I saw a flyer: "Do you think

you could laugh a woman into bed?" Although I clearly wasn't its target audience, I was intrigued, so I picked it up to have a closer look. It was advertising a six-week course on how to do stand-up comedy, culminating in a performance in the very pub where we were drinking.

I smiled. It had been quite some time since I had done a stretch activity, and this would most certainly be stretching! It would require me to put MYSELF on stage… not the armoured, professional me, but the real me. And that thought petrified me and excited me at the same time.

So, before my fear could kick in (and because I was half-cut by this point), I emailed the woman then and there to secure my place.

And so ensued the start of my Nike Year…

CHAPTER LESSONS:

- Seeking the opinion of friends and family on what you should do is great to get alternative views, but you also have to remember that their answers will come from a place that is influenced by their own mindset and experiences. If they are risk-averse and have never been in your position, they won't see the situation as you do. Unfortunately, when the risk is all yours, the decision needs to be all yours as well.
- Business partnerships can start really well, and they can often last really well. They're a funny dynamic

– a bit like a work-extended family, where you are so close and interdependent. But unlike family, you are trying to achieve something, and when your views on how you should be achieving that thing grow apart, it's a bit like a relationship breakdown heading for a divorce. Sometimes it's quick, sometimes it's slow, sometimes it's amicable… and sometimes it's not.

- Sometimes things that turn out to be your biggest turning points in life can start out as pissed-up jokes.

CHAPTER 13

Nike Year

I started the comedy course a couple of weeks after signing up. It was a small group, and I was assured by the fact that everyone seemed to be shitting themselves just as much as I was. I was still travelling away for work a lot, so would frequently take my comedy 'homework' away with me and write material in the early hours of the morning in a random hotel room somewhere, or would have a fleeting thought flash across my brain whilst driving that I would capture as a voice memo in my phone.

My brain felt like it had come alive. I was doing something completely different to my normal professional thought processes, and I was finding inspiration for material in my everyday experiences. I had started dating again, and there was no end of comedy material in those experiences (but that's a whole other book completely!), and before I knew it, the showcase night was a week away. It was scheduled for the week after my big 30th birthday party.

I hadn't exactly been relishing the thought of turning 30. If I'd told my younger self that at 30 I'd still be single, never married, no kids, barely dating, loan repayments up to my eyeballs, and working in a business that I had come to realise was driving me rather than the other way round, my younger self wouldn't exactly have been chuffed at my future prospects.

So, in the weeks leading up to my party, I made some decisions. Decisions to make the changes that I had been procrastinating on. They had been triggered by a conversation I'd had with my business partners just the week before my party. They had conceded that they needed to make changes to their business, and had asked if I would become a partner and the new Managing Director to help turn things around.

I again said I would think about it, and I did indeed consider it. For about an hour. I believed that I could turn the business round. It would be a lot of hard work, full of difficult decisions, but it was doable. Then I gave myself a reality check. Although they were asking me to be the MD, there were still three other partners. And although they said they wanted me to do this, would they actually be willing to follow through when difficult decisions were put in front of them? I wasn't convinced. And besides, I reminded myself (whilst feeling a little harsh), why should I take on a business that was hamstrung by their historical bad decisions? I didn't need that. And if I was honest with myself, although I really liked them, it wasn't me that was riding on their coat-tails.

I wanted my life back, and that started with walking away from them and the business, regardless of how far down that road we had gone. The opportunities ahead of me were more likely to be more valuable than what I would lose from walking away. And I would just have to find a way to make the loan repayments work.

I had already invited them to my party, so didn't want to have the conversation before then. To make sure that I explained myself fully, and so that I couldn't back out or be talked round, I put together an email to them, explaining my reasons and exit plan, and post-dated the send time for the day after my party. I was conscious that it was a bit of a coward's way out, but I was more than willing to talk to them about it. I just needed to explain everything rationally, without getting distracted, and for them (and myself!) to know that this was a fixed decision.

I woke up the day after my 30th birthday party and hit send, sitting back in my seat waiting tentatively for the come-back. *That's it,* I thought. *Fresh start. Now what?* I had three months to start something new and get my life back on track so that I could work towards something I DID actually want, rather than run away from something I didn't. But this time, it would be different. This time, I promised myself, I wouldn't focus on work. *No. I'm 30 now, and I can do so much more with my life. I need to stop putting things on hold for when I have more time, or more money, or a bigger house, etc. That time is now.*

This would be my Nike Year – I would "Just Do It".

Starting with my stand-up comedy. Which went AMAZINGLY! I loved every second of it, but have never been more scared in my life! The buzz I got when I came off stage made me vow to 100% do it again... when I have more time!

And so began my Nike Year. My (former) business partners weren't exactly happy about my decision, but recognised that it was mine to make. So, we severed ties and went our separate ways.

I launched my third company – a training and consultancy firm helping companies manage change by developing their HR & management practices. I reached out to my old clients and contacts, and pretty quickly picked up enough work to survive. Within about a year the work grew to a point where I needed to take on staff to keep up with the demand, and the income was through the roof.

I was designing things for big name companies, and flying round Europe to secure more work. I was busy beyond belief; on one occasion, I flew to Rome and back in a day, then out to Poland the following day to deliver some training/consulting for a new multinational client. Although, can I just say, just because this is physically possible, it doesn't mean it should be done! I said yes to everything. I had been in my stretch zone so long that I didn't spot when I had moved into my panic zone, because I was so preoccupied with telling myself that it was ok, and that I could cope. Honestly...

Unlike previous iterations, however, this time I was fixed on the fact that it wasn't all about work. I started playing tennis, after ten years off; I was going to two classes every week and trying to play a game on the weekends. The group were lovely, and I really enjoyed it. It seemed to be a stress-buster, and I would always feel better after I went. And it helped that my coach wasn't bad to look at either.

I also recognised that I had always wanted to do youth work of some kind, which was probably influenced by my mother's propensity to take in any waif and stray whilst I was growing up. I found a local charity that paired people up on a 1:1 basis to mentor disadvantaged teens, did the training, and was paired up with my first mentee.

I also realised that although it was nice to be doing well financially, I'd never been hugely driven by money. So, I offered to run employability advice sessions to my local branch of the Salvation Army, including things like CV writing, interview practice, and job connections.

And to this day, these two charitable experiences remain some of the most grounding, enlightening, and socially challenging experiences of my life. But without me realising it at the time, all of these emotional reflections planted the seed for my own not-for-profit scheme which I would go on to start years later.

As if all these activities weren't enough, I decided that I wanted a physical challenge as well. Did I decide to run a marathon, like normal people? No. Did I book a long exploratory holiday trek to far-flung lands, like normal people? No.

I decided I would climb Everest. My high-self expectations had exceeded themselves.

And so ensued a gruelling 18-month training programme. I would be away a couple of nights per week for work, still delivering training and consultancy, dropping into client sites to check in with my staff who were managing interim change projects, rushing to evening employability sessions at the Salvation Army, squeezing in 1-2 hours on the weekend to meet with my young mentee, making sure we had the cashflow to pay everybody at the end of the month, and cramming in my daily gym sessions in the early hours of the morning when I had finished a 'day's' work.

I was exhausted but fulfilled, and felt like I was finally living my promise to myself. I was indeed doing more than just work, and I was doing well from it. My income was healthy and steady, and although it wasn't always regular, I was still dating and going out with friends. I had all the boxes ticked.

I thought that maybe I had finally sorted myself out. It was the run-up to Christmas and I was looking forward to the year ahead.

But, of course… life was about to hit me on the head with a brick.

CHAPTER LESSONS:

- When you feel trapped in a world of your own making, the only person that can break you out is yourself. You may sit there and wonder whether you've invested too much time/money/effort, etc. to walk away, but as in life, it's better late than never. When I was in India, someone made a joke about another proverb – that you need to know when it's "time to sacrifice the sacred cow". I took that to mean that we need to recognise when something you have spent time and effort building no longer serves you, and it's not fair on you or anyone else to squeeze it until there is no goodwill left.

• When deciding to walk away from something, remember that it's not just about what you're leaving behind – it's about what you could have in front of you that won't happen if you don't change your circumstances. In business terms, this is referred to as the 'opportunity cost' of doing or not doing something. I had to focus on what the opportunity cost of me not pulling away was, and that gave me the strength to follow through on what was a very difficult message to deliver.

• When you're addicted to stretch and achievement, you can sometimes find yourself as a living Chinese Proverb: *if you put a frog in a pan of boiling water, it will jump straight out. But if you put it in a cold pot and heat it up slowly, it will sit there and cook.* I was cooking, but I didn't see it because I was the one turning up the heat with each new commitment.

CHAPTER 14

That Man

I was smack bang in the middle of my Nike Year, and we were in December, so I took the opportunity to convince my tennis group that we needed a Christmas get-together, as I was a little short on the 'works' parties given my self-employed status again.

I organised a dinner in a pub restaurant, where about eight of us had an absolute scream. By the time we left the restaurant, my sides were aching from all the laughter. I had already had a couple of glasses of wine, but was conscious that I should probably be doing a training session the next day, so couldn't afford to go too crazy. We moved on to a wine bar a few doors down, and ordered a couple of vodka Red Bulls to dodge the post-dinner sleepy slump and stayed there for the rest of the night, with people trailing off one by one as we crept closer to closing time.

I wasn't ready to go home (the Red Bull had kicked in!) so I tried calling a friend of mine that I figured would be in a nightclub nearby, in the hope that I could meet him rather than go home. When he didn't answer, I decided to hang on as he had a habit of keeping his phone on silent, but usually calling me back after a short while.

When the last guy from tennis finished his drink and offered to share a cab home, I explained that I was waiting to hear back from my friend, so I'd just wait. "I only live down the road anyway," I told him, "so if he doesn't call back, it'll take me ten minutes to get home. Honestly, you go. I'll see you at tennis after Christmas."

I was now the last person in the bar, which was closing up, so I called my friend again and left a message on his voicemail. "Donny, where are you? Are you out? I'm out in town and was gonna meet you in the club if you're out, so call me back and let me know." I hung up and finished what was left of my drink.

The owner of the bar came up to me just as I was reaching for my bag to leave. "Would you like another drink while you wait for your friend to call you back?" he asked. "We've closed the doors, but you can have another one while you're waiting, if you like? Rose wine was it?" He gestured to the drink I had just finished.

"Sure, why not?" I replied with a smile. It was Christmas, after all. He went to the bar and came back with a large glass of rose, then placed it on the table and gestured to the seat next to me. "Do you mind?"

I figured letting him sit with me was the least I could do, given that he didn't seem to want any money for the drink, so I nodded.

Expecting to make small talk for a while, I was surprised when he started with, "So what's a beautiful young woman like you doing out all on your own at Christmas?"

Oh dear, this may have been a mistake, I thought. *Creep alert.* I smiled tightly and replied with a short resume of my night, and took a big gulp of the wine in an attempt to keep this exchange as short as possible.

I was probably only sitting there for about 15 minutes, because I don't even remember getting to the bottom of my glass of wine…

★ ★ ★

The next thing I knew, I woke up on my bed, on top of my covers, completely naked. And my vibrator was next to me.

WHAT THE FUCK? My head was pounding and I felt groggy as fuck. I could barely move – trying to lift my arms to pull the covers over me was like moving through treacle. I winced suddenly as I moved my legs. I felt bruised and sore. Down there. And *I* didn't do that with a vibrator. I had no idea what time it was, but I just wanted to go to sleep and wake up from this as if it was a bad dream. I closed my eyes and drifted off into a black hole.

I woke again at 5pm the next day. As I pulled myself up in bed, I still felt like shit. My head was still foggy, and I was still sore. And confused. What happened? I tried to remember the night before… the last thing I remembered was being in that bar and drinking that wine…

And then I had a brief flashback... foggy, but a memory nonetheless. A memory of standing at the foot of my bed, sleepy, swaying, as that man pulled my top up over my head. I don't remember getting home. How could I not remember getting home?

Then a blank...

Think, you fucking idiot... think. What happened? My head was pounding and my whole body felt numb... and then it hit me. The last thing I remembered was lying on my bed, so sleepy I was on the verge of unconsciousness, thinking to myself, *I hope this won't take long. Just go away.* And then there was black.

Tears stung my eyes as I curled up into a tight little ball. *Did that really happen?* I questioned myself. *Surely I would remember if something like that happened?* It wouldn't be the first time I'd gotten drunk and not remembered getting home, but I'd never forget having sex with someone! Would I? And I would never sleep with that creep voluntarily. Not even if I was shit-faced! Surely? Did he drug me? Is that why I felt so shit and couldn't remember? But that's just something you hear about... it didn't happen to people I know... to people like me... surely? And even if it did, who would believe me? I wasn't even sure I believed it myself...

My mind was roaring with contradictory self-accusatory questions, indignant proclamations, and victimised shame and guilt.

How fucking stupid had I been to take a drink off someone I didn't know? I had only been five minutes down the road from my house; I should have been able to have a drink and stay safe. My mum had always warned not to take drinks off strangers, so maybe I deserved it. *Listen to your fucking mother, Sadie!*

Fuck – Mum! I had told her everything until now. How on earth could I tell her this? It would destroy her. And she would probably go to prison for killing the motherfucker. And what could I do about it anyway? I couldn't prove anything. Hell, I could barely remember it. And it'd be his word against mine. I'm guessing this wasn't the first time he'd done it – the vibrator being left out seemed some convenient staging for a "but I didn't touch you" defence. But why the fuck should he get away with it? I couldn't let him do this to someone else.

But I couldn't bring myself to do anything about it. Despite all of my armour, and all of my confident "I can handle anything bullshit", I couldn't handle this. If I told anyone, it would make it real, and I would have to handle it. And I just couldn't bring myself to do that. So, I pushed it down. Way down. Way past where the little girl was hiding, and I carried on with my life.

I carried on pretending to myself that nothing had happened. How much of a hypocrite was I? I was mentoring young girls to give them the confidence to address the injustices of their lives, and coaching professional women to speak out against unfair treatment and sexism at work. But I wasn't strong enough to do it myself.

Besides, I told myself, *I don't have time to wallow in this right now. I have too many people counting on me. Too much shit to do, and bigger things to aim for.* This happening, whether I dealt with it or not, had absolutely no bearing on any of that, so I told myself to put it to bed and plough on with life.

And that's exactly what I did.

★ ★ ★

Until now, I have still only told a handful of people about what happened. So, to those of you who know me, I'm sorry if I didn't tell you. It had nothing to do with you. I now realise that not telling people had more to do with me not wanting to deal with what happened, and the more people I told, the more likely I would have been forced/urged into doing something about it. It wasn't that I didn't trust my friends; I didn't trust *myself* to be able to handle it.

The other reason for not telling people was to avoid THAT look. That same look people gave me when I told them about what happened with Donna and Nigel. That "oh my God, poor you" look. The look of empathic woundedness that is their only way of communicating their immeasurable sympathy for you, and gratitude that it wasn't them. If I accepted "The Victim Look", it would have forced me to accept the fact that I probably should have fallen apart when it happened. Or done something about it. That those feelings which arose, but which I swiftly put in a box and buried in the vault, would have been wounding. And that was the bit I struggled with the most. That *I* was a victim. My impenetrable armour couldn't let it in – the label of "victim" seemed to be bouncing off it like two opposing magnets – yet the little girl trapped inside my armour was lurching towards it, trying to grab it as some form of comfort or validation of what had happened. I didn't know what the "normal" way to act was. I probably should have cracked, because that's what "normal" people would have done, right?

But I wasn't normal… I kept telling myself. I could cope with anything… I kept telling myself. This was no different to what I'd overcome in the past… I kept telling myself. *I'M FINE*… or so I kept telling myself.

Not telling people wasn't about them; it was about me. It was about me and my inability to accept the fact that I wasn't fine. This was another crack in my armour, and I smoothed it over with a thick layer of Polyfilla. Polyfilla on top of Polyfilla…

And that Polyfilla was work. Yet again, I threw myself into work instead of dealing with my stuff. Only occasionally did I ever allow myself to think about what happened… and even now, I still make excuses to avoid eating or drinking in that bar, or cross the street whenever I see someone ahead of me that looks like it might be him, and clench my jaw when I see his profile pop up on my internet dating apps.

The Polyfilla layers were amassing, and my way of

proving to myself the strength of my armour was to pile on even more pressure. Pressure that would end up causing an implosion.

CHAPTER LESSONS:

- As much as I hate to admit it, my mother was right. #1 Rule = never take drinks from strangers!
- It's ok to try and be strong. But when being strong becomes too big a part of how you see yourself, it can get in the way of you letting yourself struggle.
- When you "put things in a box" and don't deal with them, they might fade a bit over time, but they never go away. Someone once said to me that un-processed trauma is a bit like cooking with a dirty pan – whatever you cook will have an indeterminable taste that sours what you're trying to cook, and if you stir it up too hard you end up with little black bits floating around in your dish/life. Well, I guess nobody likes washing up, but if it means you get to avoid black bits fucking up your life later on, it's worth the effort to scrub away the emotional shit before you try to cook something new. (Although I'm not sure how a dishwasher would fit into this little analogy!)

CHAPTER 15

Take 2

My coping strategy of throwing myself into work was working. The business was growing. I, however, was exhausted – mentally and physically – but felt like I was living my promise to myself. My Nike Year had turned into more of a Nike Lifestyle.

I was earning more than double what I had ever thought possible when I started working for myself, but had become increasingly unsettled in the house since the incident at Christmas. I decided that it was time to look around and upsize on the house, so I adjusted my goalposts once again and set out on my search for the perfect next home – one without the memories that this one had.

I had also upped my time in the gym, under the auspices of boosting my training for Everest. I was usually doing an hour in the morning and again in the evening (or early hours of the morning!) every day, and it did help to keep my head relatively clear. But I had to take a rest and recovery period when I tore my calf muscle by overtraining.

It was during my recovery time, sitting on the sofa

trawling through Facebook, that I saw a post from my friend Rachel from my old course. She was looking to rent or sell her big five-bedroom Victorian house after a breakup with her partner. AND I LOVED HER HOUSE! I was sorry for her breakup, but I LOVED HER HOUSE! *That's the one for me*, I thought. Just like that, I decided I would have that house! I emailed Rachel and, after talking figures and agreeing to rent it for six months so I could get another's year trading behind me to apply for the mortgage, I rented out my own house and packed my things up, ready for the move just before the summer.

I excitedly went to meet her at the house to have a look round to see what furniture there was and what I'd need when I moved in. As I pulled up on her driveway, chatting to her on the phone, she sounded a bit hesitant. "Erm… I'm here with the letting agent," she told me. "It's Noah."

As I pulled the handbrake on, my heart skipped a beat. And when she opened the front door, I could see him standing behind her.

FUCK.

It had been just over five years, and he hadn't changed a bit. He smiled hesitantly. My thoughts immediately turned to the substantive, meaningful parts of life… *was my makeup ok?* I couldn't check now because he would see me and think I'm vain. Or still interested. *Was I still interested? Don't be stupid – he had a family now. And I'd moved on.* Well, I'd had a handful of tragically unsuccessful dates, but I COULD have met someone, and he didn't know that…

Get out of the car, Sadie, I told myself. Bracing myself, I pasted on my poker face smile and opened the car door. "Hi!" I exclaimed with as much objective, unaffected cheery vigour as I could feign, stepping out of the car and slamming the door behind me. I walked into the house and hugged Rachel whilst giving Noah a tentative smile and nod of the head. He followed suit and we had at least broken the ice.

Rachel proceeded to show me round the near-empty house, pointing out what she would be getting done before I moved in. As we walked round, I occasionally turned my head to find Noah pointing his crystal blue eyes at me and then trying to avert his gaze before I noticed.

But I did. Was this as painful for him as it was for me? *Either way, it doesn't matter*, I thought to myself. *Water under the bridge*, I told myself. *I'm not even going to think about it*, I tried to convince myself…

Rachel wrapped up the tour as we reached the front door again. She turned to Noah. "So, can you get the contract done today? I'm away for a few days and want to get it sorted before I leave. Is that ok?"

Both Noah and I stumbled, glancing at each other awkwardly. "Sure… er… why not… I'm free now, if you are?" Noah asked me tentatively.

"Yeah, of course. I can fit you in," I replied, and then could have kicked myself for the unintended pun.

"Because I don't have another appointment. I mean. I'm free now. You know what I mean." *Smooth Sadie, real smooth. You're clearly a keeper!*

I jumped in the car as we left the house and took a deep sigh of relief. I realised my body had been so tightly clenched, I felt like I had just stepped out of an electric storm with my nerves on fire. *Sort your shit out, Sadie. It's been five years. It's fine… IT'S FINE!*

I drove round the corner to his office and sat in the car for what felt like forever whilst I mustered up enough courage and composure to walk in. I swung open the door with an air of nonchalance… and tripped up the step! I managed to recover my stance before face-planting, but everyone turned and stared.

Noah laughed, with his embracing, inviting, and soothing tone. "Still making an entrance I see!" he proclaimed with a level of overfamiliarity that made my heart ache. Everyone turned back to their work as I walked to his desk at the back of the room and sat down with a deflated recognition that there was clearly still no pretence between us.

"It's nice to see you again," he said in a soft, hushed voice so nobody else would notice the undeniable tension between us. "It's been a while."

"I know," I replied. "A lot's happened," I said softly, moving my eyes to the picture of his son on the desk.

His face had a flicker of what I thought was regret, or remorse, or guilt, or something… I couldn't quite place it. But before I had much of a chance to mull it over, he pressed the professional armour switch and said, "Shall we get this contract sorted then?"

We spent the next 30 minutes going through paperwork, signing things, and softly negotiating details like the rent date and deposit, briefly forgetting our baggage and throwing in the occasional overfamiliar flirty comment like, "I know you always get what you want in the end, so I know better than to disagree with you", and "We both know you don't do the heavy lifting yourself, so you might as well put me on to the person who really runs your business!" As the meeting progressed, we laughed, we joked, and we held longing-filled silences. It felt as if I had come home again after moving away for a while. Despite my initial apprehension, I left his office secretly hoping that wouldn't be the last I saw of him again.

The next few weeks passed in a blur as I moved my stuff into Rachel's house, and cobbled together additional bits of furniture to fill the new house which was about four times the size of my small two-up, two-down end-terrace.

The summer came and went, and I celebrated moving in with a housewarming BBQ. I hoped Noah would come, but he didn't. We might have been overfamiliar, but our contact was still just about the letting arrangement. *Stop reading into things*, I scolded myself. Over the next few months, Noah and I regularly exchanged cheeky emails and calls regarding things that needed to be done around the house whilst I was renting it. I'd be lying if I didn't admit that I had a small jump of joy when something went wrong and I had an excuse to call him. And I'm pretty sure that he didn't really need to pop round and personally sort them out himself so often either.

Then Christmas came round again, and I was busy prancing round the house, having just finished putting the decorations up and polishing off one of my two 7ft Christmas trees, when my phone pinged with a text message.

It was Noah. *My car is blocked in for the lights switch-on in town. Fancy meeting me for a drink while I wait?'*

I tried my best to wait more than a millisecond to reply, but I couldn't, and walked into town quicker than my over-trained legs were fit for. He had clearly already had a couple of drinks before I got there, and I realised that he had no intention of driving home. So, why hang around? I already knew the answer, and my inner little girl warned me not to play with fire – I'd just get burned. But I didn't care. I just wanted to have a couple of hours in the company of the man who made me feel like I was whole again. And that's what I did. We sat, we drank, and we laughed. So hard that people stared.

I was having the time of my life when the bar called last orders. My heart sank. "You should probably be making your way home now then, I guess," I told him. "In a taxi, of course!"

"Absolutely," he said. "Right after I walk you home."

GULP. It was just a walk home. Nothing in it. It was fine. We were both adults. It would be fine.

146

We walked back to my house, with a few slightly heavy, awkward, unspoken pauses. There was definitely an elephant in the room, and I had no idea whether we would talk about it or not. So, finally, I threw it out there… "Do you want to come in and talk?" I asked.

He nodded and in we went. I poured us a drink and we both stood there awkwardly. "This is so weird," I said. Then we just laughed at the bizarreness of the situation, and the ice felt like it had been broken.

We spent the next few hours talking: about the past; about unfinished business; and about the future. At some point, things moved beyond just talking, and I remember feeling a heightened mix of relief and contentment, tainted with a spattering of anxiety and foreboding. *Did this make me the other woman now? Was I breaking up a family? If he wasn't happy, then it was his right to leave. It's not healthy to stay in an unhappy relationship. Did I cause this? What next?* It all felt so complicated. I didn't want to be the other woman, but I didn't want to stop. I felt like the past five years had just been erased and we had picked up where we left off.

The confusing mix of indignant justifications and self-deprecating reflections were churning in my head well into the next day, and the day after, and the day after that. But it didn't stop Noah and I stealing every moment we could together. Coffee shops. Shopping centres. Museums. Anywhere we could pretend that it was just us. To pretend that life was simple.

Shortly after we had started seeing each other, Noah

had moved out and was sleeping on a friend's sofa whilst looking into flats. He clearly had a heavy heart, and the last thing I wanted was to see him in pain, even though I was the thing that was inducing that pain. He was missing his son desperately, but said he was happier now he was moving forward.

Noah had told Joan about us when he moved out, and she obviously wasn't pleased but hadn't seemed surprised. After Christmas, he agreed to have counselling with her to find a way to work out how they would co-parent their son following the break-up. And I went into a mini-meltdown. Couples' therapy? Despite his assurances that it was with a view to moving on, I had my concerns. He had gone back to her once before – what was to say he wouldn't again?

When he was officially single, we stepped things up a notch and often took his son out for the day somewhere, playing happy families. For those few hours, the world seemed whole again. Then Joan would call, or we would bump into someone he knew, and that deeply conflicted look would reappear on his face, and my inner little girl would curl up into a self-protecting little ball. Even though he was single and Joan knew about us, he still obviously felt a draw back to his family life. And I got that. I wanted him to be the kind of man that put his family first, but he also deserved to be happy, right? I was conflicted, and I couldn't do anything about it.

So, I did what I always did – I distracted myself from the pressure of dealing with that situation by piling on the pressure of another situation. My brother had decided that he wanted to rent out his flat for some extra money, and as I had loads of room in my place, he moved in with me. But instead of saying, "You're an adult, you can manage that, but I'm here to support you", I tasked myself with managing his move, refurbing his flat, and finding him new tenants.

At the same time, my mum retired from her job, but was clearly struggling to make the adjustment into retired life, not knowing what to do with herself, and trying to get by on her State pension. Rather than say, "You're an adult, you can sort that out, but I'm here to support you", I offered her a job in my company, doing telesales to book me appointments and securing me sponsorship for my Everest trip.

I had just piled another load of distractions on top of my already hectic schedule, and my Tetris time management skills were being tested beyond belief. However, it did stop me dwelling on the things I couldn't control, like Noah's therapy sessions with Joan. Instead, I was worrying about financially floating most of my family, and how I would fit in a trip to my brother's flat to let in the carpet guys in-between four conference calls and a new business proposal.

One day, I was sitting in my car, parked outside my brother's flat, typing away on my laptop to finish a proposal. I'd just finished one conference call and was waiting for three minutes to pass before dialling into my second. The carpet guys were late, but that was fine – I could let them in if I muted the next call. I hopped on the next call, and looked at my watch. I also had to be at the hardware store to get keys cut before it closed. Where the fuck were the carpet guys? My third call finished, and I dialled into my fourth, which only lasted a couple of minutes.

I hung up and dialled the carpet guys. They'd forgotten, and would be out tomorrow instead. "I CAN'T DO TOMORROW!" I yelled down the phone and hung up, bursting into tears. *What the fuck is wrong with me?* I asked myself. *I'm not this person. I don't shout at people. I never lose my temper.* I wiped my nose and went home. The hardware shop had already closed. Fabulous. Just my luck.

I'd been in the house about six months now, so Rachel and I began having valuations carried out in readiness for me to buy it. We were struggling to find a middle ground between what the valuations said and what she needed to sell for, which was another thing on my mind. I loved the house. It had so much potential as a family home (even though I'd never actually set my sights on having a family); the coach-house at the end of the garden would be a perfect space for Mum when she didn't want to live on her own any more (even though it was dilapidated and needed rebuilding); and the property had so much potential (even though it needed a lot of money spending on it, and most of my cash was tied up in the company and its staffing bill).

Reluctantly, I decided to bite the bullet and agree

with Rachel that it was probably best she looked for another buyer, then I spoke to Noah about finding me somewhere else to rent while I found the right place to buy. I was disappointed but figured it might be for the best. Although I wasn't sure how I would survive my second house move within 12 months.

By this point, it was mid-January. Noah and I hadn't been back together for long, but it felt like it was just meant to be. He found a house and asked me to meet him there one afternoon.

"Just remember, it's not a forever home – just a stepping-stone," he told me as he unlocked the front door, "but it might be perfect for right now.

He pointed out the driveway, which could fit three cars; the open-plan living room, which was ideal for family dining; the downstairs bedroom which would be great for my brother (he was coming with me for now!) or an office later; the upstairs master bedroom, which had an en-suite; and the small third bedroom, painted blue and perfect for little boys.

I looked at him as he looked back at me. *Had we just had a conversation about this being a "family" home?* I wondered. "Not right now, but you know…" he said with a shrug of his shoulders. I smiled. Maybe all of my worries about this couples' counselling had been unwarranted.

The next day, I signed for the house and started packing up my stuff. Within a couple of weeks, I had moved in, conscious that I needed to get settled before my mid-February ice climbing trip to the Alps, which was in preparation for my April departure for Everest.

The house was piled with boxes, but I wasn't interested in sorting anything out until Noah had been round and discussed where the furniture, etc, would go. He arrived about 7pm the day I moved in, and I could immediately see he was distracted. He brushed it off with an excuse about work, but I had a familiar feeling rising inside me, especially when he ignored his buzzing phone a few times, saying it was an annoyingly persistent tenant. I tried to distract him with a cheeky invitation to come upstairs and "see what I had done with my wardrobes" and he laughed, following me up.

We ended up in the shower, and I still remember it as one of the most intense moments of my life. That little 2ft-square cubicle seemed to contain as much concentrated electrified chemistry as a lightning storm in a safe. It was like something out of a movie, and I had never felt so powerfully connected to someone in my life. It was different to anytime before, but I immersed myself in his embrace rather than question why.

I decided to surprise him at work the next day with some coffee and cake. As I walked in through the door, rather than be greeted by the beaming smile and sparkling eyes I was used to, a shadow fell across his face. I stopped in my tracks. "What's wrong?" I asked anxiously. I was starting to sound like a broken record.

"I'm sorry. I'm just busy and I don't have time for this right now," he said dismissively. "I'll call you later."

I started to turn back with my tail between my legs, then changed my mind and whipped back round again. I have never been one to shy away from a difficult conversation, so despite my concerns at his possible answer, I decided that I wouldn't let him dodge this conversation. It wasn't fair to keep me hanging, and I deserved to know what was going on.

"Can I speak to you outside, please?" I asked, with a tone that clearly said I wasn't going anywhere without some kind of a conversation. He conceded, picking up his packet of cigarettes. He knew I hated smoking, as my mum had done it for years, so I took this as a passive "fuck you" gesture.

"What's going on, Noah?" I asked outside. "And don't just say that it's work, because I'm not stupid. Don't go cold turkey on me again – I deserve better!" I said firmly, trying to hold back tears.

He took a long hard drag on his cigarette and exhaled slowly. "I know. I'm sorry, but it's so complicated. Someone's going to get hurt, and I just don't know what to do about it. It's easy for you, all you've got to worry about is your dog. I've got a bit more to consider." It was as though this was the first time he had considered leaving, despite having moved out months before.

"What do you mean someone *is going to* get hurt? I thought you had already made your decision?" I countered. "I've just rented a fucking house, Noah…"

"I just don't know what to do," he said, blowing out another long puff of smoke.

The tears started to sting my eyes, and I couldn't think of what to say, so I turned and walked back to my car as quickly as I could before my mascara hit the deck. *What the fuck?* I asked myself. *I thought we were good?*

I called him later that night, but he didn't respond. Or the next day. My mind was whirling with thoughts: *Had I done something wrong? What had happened? I'd thought we were doing well… This couldn't be it right now.*

The next day, I had an appointment booked at the doctor's to talk about getting some altitude sickness tablets, which is where this story began in Chapter 1. And you know how that went! On my way out of the appointment, with my tissue glued to my streaming nose, my self-deprecating thoughts were reeling. *It's no fucking wonder he's thinking of leaving you – you're a fucking mess*, I told myself. *I mean, what could possibly make this situation any worse…*

And then I stopped… in the middle of the doctor's waiting room… I'M LATE! No, that would be ridiculous. And impossible. I had a coil fitted. I was covered. That's why I was irregular. I was sure of it.

But just in case, I picked up a pregnancy test whilst I was waiting for my anti-depression tablets. I couldn't wait, so went back into the doctor's toilet to do it. It was positive. FUCK. *I can't have a baby,* I thought. *I'm supposed to be going up Everest. And what if Noah leaves me? I'm not even sure I want kids of my own…*

My head was whirring as I drove away from the doctor's surgery. I don't know what made me do it, but instead of going home, I went to Noah's office. He was standing outside smoking when I pulled up outside. And yet again, he didn't look pleased to see me.

"I've just been to the doctor's…" I began.

His face fell, and in that instant, I had a *Sliding Doors* moment. I could tell him I was pregnant, but then his decision to stay or go would be influenced by his overcharged duty to do what he thought was the right thing. Which I was pretty sure was how he and Joan had ended up together in the first place, and look how that turned out? Or I could not tell him, and hope that he would make the decision to stay with me of his own accord.

The words fell out of my mouth. "She said I have depression."

"Well, you do have a lot on at the moment," he retorted, with a painful lack of empathy.

We exchanged a few other bits of inconsequential small talk, and I got back in my car with a tentative "speak to you later" farewell. Then I drove home to commence the foetal position you became familiar with in Chapter 1.

Should I have told him? I guess we'll never know…

CHAPTER LESSONS:

• Before Noah, I would never have thrown myself at a relationship as fully as I did here. NEVER. But because I had so much instability in other areas of my life, I saw what was unfinished business as my second chance of happiness, and I threw everything I had at it. Where your head is at in life will inevitably have a big impact on how you see the world and the people you meet. I felt lonely from going self-employed, and then met Noah. Without realising it, I decided that he was everything I was missing in life. As much as we got on really well, if I hadn't felt a sense of lack, would I have attached so quickly in the cold light of day? I'm pretty sure my loneliness caused me to view our connection with heavily rose-tinted glasses.

- Noah didn't break me. *I* broke me, because I hung all of my hopes of happiness on him, and I focused on *him* being the event that would 'fix' me and my life. It wasn't his job to fix me – it was my job to fix me, but I missed the signs and he was just the straw that broke the camel's back.

CHAPTER 16

Strike 3

The next few days were a blur. I remember waking up and wanting the world to go away, so I turned over and closed my eyes again. The only safe space for me right now was my bed. My phone kept buzzing – my staff wondered where I was, they wanted to check in and clarify questions, but I couldn't face anything, so I turned my phone off.

I had dodged as many of the calls from my mother as I could, but she wasn't taking the unavailable tone for an answer and turned up at my door. I told her about Noah, and she hugged me. I told her about the doctor's, and she squeezed me. Then she set about fixing things in the only way she knew how – she made me an omelette.

My father and brother followed suit, after she shared the news with them. Both regularly checked in with me, only to be met with a weak smile and a shrug of the shoulders in an unspoken "time to move on, darling" gesture.

I felt like I had fallen off my pedestal, and the wind had been well and truly knocked out of me. The life I had engineered for myself had turned into a prison of my own making, and I had no idea how to escape. I didn't know which way to turn or even which way was up. It was almost as if someone had removed my life's north star, and all of a sudden I had no way of navigating my way forward. I felt stuck. And dark. So very, very dark.

My friends and family popped round to check in on me. I tried to explain what was swarming around in my head, but the thoughts and feelings seemed too slippery for me to grasp hold of long enough to find the words to describe them. "I don't know what to do with myself. I know that I've stretched myself for far too long, but if I don't stretch and strive, then who am I?" I'd tell them. I felt like I had lost my identity, that there wasn't much of me beneath the work and the challenges and the achievements and the constant stretch.

On some level I recognised that I had been self-medicating for a while, distracting myself from things I couldn't control with things I could, like work, and change, and achievement. I was an addict... an achievement addict. I was incapable of not stretching, because if I stood still for too long, I would realise that all of this was purely a way of numbing the fact that I was unhappy. That I didn't know what I actually wanted. I was an unhappy overachiever.

My company was hugely successful, but it didn't make me happy. I felt like I was being managed by it, not the other way round. And my team were lovely, but my work was taking me further and further away from doing the frontline things I loved. Instead of helping people with my training and consulting, it had become an anonymous, meaningless activity. And a financial burden.

I loved my family, but I had assumed the role of the family matriarch and lost all sense of boundaries of what was and wasn't my responsibility to fix.

So, I needed to make some dramatic changes. I knew that, but these things just seemed too big to know where to start. Instead, I spent my time lying on the sofa, watching daytime TV, and drifting in and out of the blackness in my head.

One of the biggest challenges I faced was that being self-employed, I couldn't just take time off sick. After a couple of days, I had to dust myself off and show my face at a client site for a big meeting. I was managing the merger of a small group of doctors' surgeries, and their timescales didn't allow for me having a breakdown. I put my armour back on and steadied myself for the meeting.

I managed to paste on enough of a robotic presence to make it through the meeting, but was wiping my eyes in the bathroom afterwards when one of the staff caught me. Luckily, it was a woman I got on with really well, who was also the practice nurse.

"Can I ask a favour?" I asked tentatively. "Can you do me a pregnancy test?" She could see that I didn't want to talk about it, so she took me to her treatment room, gave me the test, and took it back off me after I'd visited the loo. After a few minutes, she looked at me over the rim of her glasses. "It's negative," she told me, then added, "Is that good or bad?"

I was relieved, to say the least, but also conflicted. Even though I didn't really want kids, I felt like I had lost something. And I felt a little guilty for feeling relieved.

So, that was that then… it really was the end of things with Noah. On one hand, I was glad not to have ties with a man who ultimately didn't want me. But on the other hand, I couldn't help but wonder whether telling him would have made any difference to his decision. Either way, I wasn't actually pregnant, and mulling over "what ifs" wasn't going to help me. I put it in a mental box and tucked it safely away in my brain's filing cabinet, with all the other unresolved issues. At least that was one less thing I had to worry about.

Two weeks had passed, and the doctor wanted to see me again to find out about my progress on the tablets. I just about managed to get up and shower before making it there, although I did burst into tears when my conditioner ran out; it seemed like the end of the world at that moment in time. I filled in the little form again, without showing much improvement for my desire to re-join the world, so she upped my tablets. "Just give it time," she urged me, as I left her office with a long face.

The weeks turned into months, and I was just about surviving, doing whatever work I had to, and keeping work ticking over with the bare minimum, but I knew I needed to make some changes. When I wasn't out of the house working, I was still spending my time in the comfortable cocoon of my sofa. Eventually, my brother decided to address this by dragging me out with him and his friends at every opportunity, but I would sit there quietly, watching as everybody around me talked and laughed, as if they were operating on a completely different frequency from me. I smiled politely when prompted, and participated in conversations when required, but felt like a lonely outsider, even when surrounded by people who loved me. Years later, my brother told me that it was as though I had been "lobotomised" during that time; it's funny how the way you think you are and the way you actually come across can be so different. I thought I was just going around like a miserable bitch; everyone else thought I was a shell of a person.

I'd return to the house that I had rented with me and Noah in mind, and just stare at the boxes. I couldn't bring myself to unpack, and would walk past the spare room that would never be used, and just crawl into the safety of my bed.

Then one day I decided to open the curtains when I got up. I honestly don't know what prompted me; maybe it was a sunny day or something. But I looked out of the window and saw some kids playing in the close… and I smiled. I don't think I had smiled instinctively (one that wasn't pasted on or forced as a sign of social inclusion) for a long time. And instead of scraping my hair up and spending the day in my PJs, I washed and dried my hair, got dressed, and put on makeup. It was a Saturday morning and my friend Vicky was coming over, and when I opened the door to her it was obvious that she was pleasantly surprised to see I looked more human than I had of late.

"You look nice," she made a point of saying as I let her in. I made us a cuppa and we took a seat on my trusty sofas. "So, what are your plans this weekend?" she asked, making polite small talk. I stopped and thought carefully. This was the first weekend that I had actually felt a slight desire to do something, but I genuinely had no idea what to do.

"I don't know," I replied eventually. "What do normal people do on weekends instead of work?" It sounded like a stupid question, but it had genuinely been so long since I had spent any time doing leisurely things instead of work that I had no idea where to start. She just laughed and we spent about an hour making a list of things I could do, and things I wanted to do to make myself feel better – like moving the boxes from off my dining table and into the garage. It wasn't exactly unpacking, but it eased the pang of darkness when I didn't have to look at them every day. After she left, I spent an hour browsing Amazon for self-help books on coping with depression, stress, and breakdowns, and how to identify what you wanted to do with your life.

Part of my treatment plan with the doctor was to have some sessions with a psychologist. I had only had one session, but it gave me a surprising amount of clarity.

It turns out that I had, for whatever reason, what she referred to as Rescuer Syndrome. This is where I saw someone with a problem and took it upon myself to fix it for them. To the point where it would break me. This insight gave me the stark wake-up call I needed. That is why I had moved my brother into my house; why I was employing my mum; why I was probably employing people I didn't really need. I was distracting myself from fixing *me*, by trying to fix *them*.

I needed to make some changes, and I needed to make them now. So, I spent that entire weekend deciding what I wanted to do about my life and what changes I wanted to make. I checked them with friends, as the first things doctors tell you when you are given a depression diagnosis is NOT to make any life-altering decisions until you feel better. And I wanted to make sure that I wasn't looking to make more change just for change's sake.

First things first. The doctor had pretty much made the decision for me, but I had to formalise it. I emailed my expedition organisers and notified them that I would be pulling out of the Everest trip. I expected to feel like I'd let myself down, but all I felt was relief. That surprised me, because I clearly hadn't let any true feelings enter my head for a long time now, and that one took me by surprise.

Secondly, this house had to go. I registered with estate agents and spoke to a broker about a new mortgage application. I wanted to set down roots and get some stability back in my life. And I could do that with sensible aspirations that didn't stretch me over budget for a huge house that I wouldn't be filling any time soon.

Thirdly, I wanted out of work! I wanted to close down my company and start afresh; it felt like it didn't matter any more, and I had had enough. My friend, Sarah, talked me out of this one. "Don't kneejerk," she said, "it's an overreaction. Just downsize so you can get back to just doing the things you love." So, that's what I did.

I took a deep breath and let ALL of my staff go, along with the parts of work that I didn't really enjoy doing, and took it right back to just me doing what I wanted to do. This, like before, felt like a massive failure, but I recognised that it was the right decision to make for me at that point in time. And although I still didn't feel like what I was doing was earth-shatteringly important in the world, I could cope with carrying on with it until I decided what I DID actually want to do with my life.

And fourthly, I needed to make small changes that would make me more mindful of what was good and bad for my head. I made a list of all the things that made me feel better, and all the things that made me feel worse, and stuck it on the door of my fridge. I gave my friends and family a copy of the list, and gave them permission to hold me to account for it. I also promised myself to do at least two of the good things each day – some as simple as just putting on my best lacy pants in the morning – if I felt down, and to call my friends if I had the urge to cocoon on the sofa and hide in a boxset on a weekend.

The big one that I specifically asked all of my friends and family to hold me to account for was that I should not commit to any 'stretch' projects or changes until I found my feet again. So, other than the house move, everything else was off the table. No exciting projects, no new business ideas, no big distractions. I had to start learning how to be JUST ME. I had to learn how to coast in order to get back a realistic feeling of what a normal level of stress and pressure looked like.

It reminded me of that old fable about the frog and the hot water. I had been baking for quite some time and forgotten what a healthy water temperature was. Taking my foot off the pedal *a bit* wouldn't help, because although it would slow me down, I would still have been going way over the speed limit due to how far I had pushed myself. Nope, I had to go cold turkey and start from scratch.

This was complicated. If you're an alcoholic, you know when you're drinking and you're not. There are even warnings on labels like mouthwash to help you avoid any accidental slip-ups. But being a business owner, it wasn't quite so simple to go cold turkey on the stretch and achievement opportunities. Decisions were all around me, and I had no clear way of deciding which ones were inside my new cold turkey boundaries and which ones weren't. And sitting in a self-proclaimed world of bland nothingness wouldn't exactly be good for my depression either.

I had to develop my own little mind test: what was the reason I was interested in this new opportunity/ what was the reason I wanted to make this decision? Was it because I could? Was it because it was exciting and unknown? Was it because it was shiny and new? Was it because it would fill a gaping hole for me? If it was something that a "normal" person would take on, or something that my friends and family would say was acceptable, then I could do it. If not, the answer had to be no. I basically shifted my car into neutral and gave others the steering wheel to direct me.

I felt passive, though, and I hated the fact that I was coasting. But I didn't know what else to do. In the end, I just kept putting on my best lacy pants and hoped for the best!

I would love to say that something amazing happened, that I had a turnaround moment, or that making these changes was revolutionary. But it wasn't. There were no quick fixes for me, and although I gradually got better, bit by bit feeling like I was piecing myself back together, it just took time. And perseverance. And faith... Faith that I could fix me, and that there was something worth fixing me for.

And there was, but it would take me a while to find it. This may have been my third strike, but I was not out of the game yet...

CHAPTER LESSONS:

- "It's not how many times you get knocked down that count, it's how many times you get back up." George A Cluster

- When you're in a dark place, it can seem like the expanse in front of you is full of nothingness. And how can you move forward when you have no navigational markers to guide you about which is the best way forward? I had NO idea what I wanted next or where I was going – I just knew I didn't want to stay where I was. So, just focus on your single next step. Not the whole route – that's overwhelming, or worst case, too faint to see. Just do SOMETHING that helps you take one single step forward, and as those steps build up, the fog starts to lift, and you start to see navigational markers begin to emerge. Basically, your path only becomes clear when you are in motion. Just do SOMETHING, and the rest will work itself out.

- When I downsized my company back to just me, I felt like a MASSIVE failure. I'd let people down that were counting on me, and I thought I must be CRAZY for ruining a profitable business. But I didn't want to be successful at something that didn't matter to me. As my mindset changed, so did my priorities.

CHAPTER 17

An Unexpected Lesson

In the grand scheme of things, I was on anti-depressants for about 18 months, and still finding my mojo for six months after that. The initial changes I made did help, as did the little daily habits and promises I made to myself as they switched my brain's way of working from dark to light.

I engaged with a life coach to help me identify what I wanted in life, to help me keep track of my self-care routine, and make sure I didn't get sucked into my world of work and overcommitment again.

I'd re-focused on what was important, and was spending much more time with family and friends. I had returned to seeing my parents every weekend, and was back to speaking to Mum almost daily. She had since settled into retired life a bit more comfortably and no longer needed me to employ her, which took the financial burden off, as well as the awkward conversations about whether it was appropriate for your employee to be drinking gin and tonic at 11am just because the tonic would go flat otherwise! And instead of giving her a strict 15-minute supermarket shopping slot to fit in with my other commitments, we would take a day out during the week to go somewhere new or for a boozy lunch somewhere.

Over time, I became less snappy, more engaged, and generally a much nicer person to be around. And it helped that I had found my dream home a couple of months after my break-up with Noah. Dealing with his office, whilst avoiding him directly to manage the lease on the house, was a stressful challenge I could have done without, but I was now officially settled into my new life, and my fresh start was taking root.

However, I was still coasting. Work was ticking over, but I was becoming increasingly bored and disenfranchised, and I needed to review my promise of not committing to anything stretching. I had bedded in the basics of a new, healthy life, and now wanted to work on what would make me happy. I needed something to work towards again.

So, I focused my coaching sessions on what I DID want out of life, and despite the fact that I had increasingly decided that I didn't really want children, I did still have a social urge to do something that was bigger than me. I had taken a short break in my youth mentoring while I was recovering, but had since started to help a second young girl who had a difficult home background, and I found it really fulfilling. If I didn't have my own kids, it didn't mean I couldn't help someone else's, right?

I decided to look into fostering. Supported Lodging fostering, to be specific; helping a teenager about to come out of the care system to live more independently almost as a housemate, but with more parental-style guidance to help them grow into their independence.

And true to form, once I had set my sights on it, it was a done deal. I enrolled, and started the training and screening process. It was enlightening and terrifying at the same time, but I felt like a part of me had been switched on for the first time ever.

I was nearing the final stages of the approval process when I received a phone call one day. The girl that I had been mentoring had decided that she wasn't going home again now that she had hit 16. She wanted a new life, and asked if I could help her find somewhere to live. Ok, my rescuer syndrome kicked in. She had very few other people on her side, so I did everything I could to help her find her feet. We got her into a small, young women's shared residence, but she got herself kicked out of there. She then got into a slightly less nice, larger, shared residence, and started carrying round a knife so she would feel safe, then got kicked out of there for not following the rules. She was nosediving, and Social Services couldn't help because she wasn't engaging with the system. One day, she was put up in emergency accommodation that was a sheltered adults' B&B, where you had to lock yourself into your room due to the "issues" of some of the other residents.

Enough was enough. I was aware that it was way beyond my responsibility, but I had a spare room, and I couldn't sit back and watch a 16-year-old girl end up on the streets when I had a perfectly good bed at home. I pulled out of the fostering process and moved her in with me, in the hope that a more stable base might help with some of the risk-taking decision-making patterns.

And it did. She was there for six months, and for at least the first half of it we jostled on a few ground rules, but she responded well. It was a bizarre relationship that switched from a quasi-adult:child dynamic to friend:friend in a single conversation, but we muddled our way through with only a small handful of fallouts.

The challenge came when we started working on her "next steps". I was very clear with her that she could stay with me as long as we worked on her future choices so that she could eventually stand on her own two feet, and she agreed. And when it came to looking at jobs, she progressed to the final stages of the interview process, then didn't turn up at the final stage. Lots of reasons ensued, along with promises of trying again, but not much follow-through. Then her rent stopped, because she wasn't filling in her benefits paperwork. Then she stopped coming home every night, avoiding me for days to dodge an accountability conversation.

It seemed like the harder I pushed her to make sustainable decisions, the harder she pushed back and made risky decisions. And it was heart-breaking to watch. In the end, although we were ok in our general relationship with each other, I think we both recognised her need to move on. She decided she would move in with her boyfriend, which I recognised as her choice to make as an adult, albeit with a few "are you sure this is the best decision?" prompts thrown into the conversations.

I caught up with her a handful of times for dinner or coffee after she moved out, but things petered out when she would forget or cancel at the last minute. I hated to let go, but although I recognised that my rescuer syndrome had already stepped in more than it should have done, I also recognised that you can only take a horse to water. So, I let her know that I would always be there if she needed me, and she knew where I was if she wanted to catch up, but I would leave it up to her to let me know when she was around.

And that was the last I saw of her for about five years. I had the occasional message from her to say hi, and how she had had to overcome a few life challenges, but then I saw her about five years later and learned that she and the same boyfriend were having a baby. I hope that she is happy, and that her life is now as she would want it.

Although my time with her was one of the most difficult experiences of my life, it actually gave me a really unexpected lesson that I didn't spot at the time. A lesson that would go on to shape one of the biggest achievements of my life. One that would enable me to balance my Rescuer Syndrome with healthy boundaries AND satisfy my need for achievement. All whilst changing the world for one young person at a time!

CHAPTER LESSONS:

- Sometimes, the hardest lessons in life are actually just training to help you do things that you wouldn't be able to if it weren't for those moments.

- You can take a horse to water, but you can't make it drink. If that horse walks away from the water, following it around and trying to convince it to stay hydrated won't change a thing! Sometimes you have to wait for that horse to get thirsty, then just be there for them at the water's edge.

- When you spot that there is something missing in your life, remember that there is usually more than one way to fill that gap. Some options could take you down another thorny route if you lurch towards them too quickly. In hindsight, I'm actually really glad that I didn't progress with the fostering process at that point. If I had, I wouldn't have learnt this lesson so quickly, and later had the capacity to go on to do what I am now with my youth project, which is helping many more young people than I would ever have through fostering.

CHAPTER 18

Eureka Moment

I had been living in my new house for about a year, and finally felt like myself again (or rather, I felt like the new me. I had been flogging myself for so long I'm not sure that "going back" to the old me was really an option.). But, although I felt ok in myself, I was still coasting. Work was ok, but it didn't set me on fire. My life was ok, but it felt a bit beige. I still wanted to do extraordinary things, but wasn't sure how I could do that without damaging myself.

Then, on one unexceptional day, in the early hours of the morning, I awoke with a start. I was suddenly wide awake, and my mind was buzzing around a number of observations I had recently made:

I had recently designed and delivered a training course on the future of work trends, and had spent a lot of time researching how the self-employment movement looked to be an unstoppable global trend.

I had also done some work with the Salvation Army to help their homeless hostel residents develop some employability skills, and had seen the massive confidence boost they got from working in the in-house social enterprises that they run.

In my capacity as a youth mentor, I had worked alongside a number of other youth development agencies, and noted that most of them did some real good but stopped short of actually placing tangible opportunities in front of the teens for them to grasp and move forward with. So, when the services finished, the youngsters often fell back into wherever they came from.

I was frequently working with clients who were increasingly complaining that the young people they were recruiting didn't have any real-life skills, confidence, or proactivity when they started work, AND that they needed their more established staff to be more entrepreneurial.

Having worked with a few disenfranchised teens who had completely disengaged with the education system, or were frequent attenders at the Jobcentre, I started to wonder if there was another way to dangle a carrot to get these youngsters engaged.

And I had been thinking for some time that although I had clearly gone too far with it, my self-employment journey had taken me to heights and taught me things that I never would have experienced (or at least as quickly as I had) if I had stayed in a mainstream employment pathway.

I swung my legs over the side of the bed and put on my slippers and dressing gown before racing downstairs, nearly tripping over my dog who was sleeping on her back outside my bedroom door. There were jumbled thoughts swimming around in my head, and I could feel my neurons firing, starting to join up the dots…

I fished out a bunch of flipchart papers, Post-It notes, and coloured markers, and began to extract the thoughts swirling round my head. By the time I had finished, my kitchen walls looked like the inside of an asylum cell, with the filled flipcharts Blu Tacked to the walls and the Post-It notes flaking off and floating to the floor! Yet I had the feeling that something special was forming…

I had basically brought together a number of the thoughts I'd had and things that I had seen, to roughly sketch a new concept. One that would use a not-for-profit social enterprise to teach young people how to become self-employed, but would at the same time act as an engagement mechanism for hard-to-reach youngsters (with the potential to earn their own money as the carrot), as well as develop a range of transferable employability skills, like proactivity, self-accountability, and entrepreneurialism – all of which can't really be taught, but must be experienced to learn.

My initial idea was that I would set up a youth development project and run a range of enterprise challenges (similar to *The Apprentice* TV show) where young people could gain real experience of setting up and running their own business in a range of different skills and sectors. They wouldn't be "trained" or "taught" the theory of entrepreneurialism; they would live the behaviours by learning as they went along, and working alongside real professionals. The project would grow into brokering work experience placements and launching trading youth enterprises as a next step, to help them go on to try their hand in related roles if they found something they liked. And ultimately, we could help them set up their own businesses if they were interested.

So, at 3am one day in 2014, my brainchild was born. I didn't know what it would be called, but I knew what I wanted it to look like.

I wanted to help young people carve their own path in the world, and in order to do so, I would have to carve my own path, because this was a completely different model to anything I was aware of. And it was a BIG undertaking! I had NO idea how to run a not-for-profit scheme. And I had NO youth development contacts. And I had NO experience of running a youth development scheme. Perfect. Should be easy then...

Despite ALL of the challenges, I felt like something had just lit up inside me. And although I had no idea where to start, I felt as if this was too important to not do. I believed that I would find a way. I had to.

I decided to be brave and make a start. I was acutely aware of my complete lack of experience and credibility in this arena, so was really nervous sharing my thoughts on what I wanted to do. I was worried people would tell me I was naive, that I didn't know what I was doing, and that it wasn't possible. Or that they might steal my idea if they didn't think it was a load of bollox. But I figured this wasn't going to happen if it stayed inside my head, so I took a deep breath and introduced it to the world.

To start with, I struggled to explain it to the world (the above description took some time to clarify!), but the intention of using self-employment skills as a way of developing and engaging teens was clear, and the people I spoke to in my immediate network were really interested. They gave me names of other people I should speak to. I emailed them, and had more meetings. I even managed to drum up a couple of people who were interested in volunteering to help me get things off the ground. In fact, the reception to the concept was overwhelmingly positive. "But how will you make it happen?" they asked. "I have absolutely no fucking idea," I replied, "but I'm sure I will find a way!"

I began to look around for people that had, like me, made the leap from the corporate world and launched a youth development project/scheme/company. After asking around, I came across a local guy who had done just that. I got in touch, explained my idea to him over email, and asked if he would be willing to meet with me to share how he got his operation off the ground. I also asked if he might mentor me a little, so that I could better understand the not-for-profit sector. I hit send and waited with bated breath.

He eventually came back to me, saying that unfortunately he thought mentoring me might be a conflict of interest because he couldn't promise that they wouldn't look to do something similar in the future. It wasn't the response I had expected; I hadn't appreciated how competitive the not-for-profit sector might be in itself. But I chalked it down to experience and moved on. I later learnt that this man (unsuccessfully!) pitched my idea to his own trustee board, which made me realise that, charity or not, sometimes snakes in the grass lurk in the most virtuous places!

It took me about six months, and conversations with a LOT of people, until I finally felt ready to move my idea forward. It was time to name this beast! I jotted down a load of company names that seemed related: Project Launchpad, Springboard, Phoenix, Go Your Own Way, and a whole load of others. Then I set about figuring out what was available as a legal company name, domain names, social media handles, etc. Everything was taken. Fuck. It would appear that I wasn't as original as I had hoped!

Then it came to me… I wanted to give young people a platform to find what they loved, learn how to do it, and to leap into the world of the unknown. I typed my name idea into my laptop – the limited company name, website domain, and social media handles were available! I secured the name, purchased the URL, set up the sites, filled in the paperwork, and sketched a logo. And so, The Platform Project was born in 2015.

I was determined that this would be a not-for-profit company (rather than have profit shares or be a charity), so I set it up as a Community Interest Company. My accountant nearly fell off his chair when I told him that I didn't want to make any money out of it – but it just didn't feel right. What I wanted was to run the project as a financially sustainable company, rather than a charity that was reliant on funding all the time. If I was preaching to the young people that they should be entrepreneurial and financially sustainable, it only seemed right that the company should be as well. However, I did recognise that I would need some funding to get it off the ground, so I eagerly put in a funding application for £150,000 to launch the scheme as a full-time company undertaking… and swiftly got turned down.

FUCK! I had no proof that my idea would work, no operational history to show I could make it work, no results to show that the funding would actually make a difference in the world, no financial track record, and no policies or procedures. I had basically done the equivalent of going to a bank and asking for loads of money, with no way of proving that my business would work or that they stood any chance of getting their investment back. My idea was not naive, but my initial approach certainly had been.

I was as impatient as ever and wanted everything to happen immediately, but realised that I didn't have the opportunity to force this along as I had with previous business projects. I would need to find another way to get it off the ground. Again, I had absolutely no idea how or when, but I was resolute that it would 100% happen.

Little did I know that by the end of the year my life would change in a way that would make me drop this project like it had never even mattered.

CHAPTER LESSONS:

- Ideas usually only start turning into action when you start talking to people about them. You will always come across assholes who try to poo-poo your idea or steal it (or both!). Don't go into protective mode and over-incubate your idea – you WILL kill it. It needs to see light to grow. And don't worry about the assholes – YOU are your competitive advantage, because YOU have been mulling this idea around for ages, whereas they have just seen the tip of the iceberg.

- Doing anything different is scary. I had already started multiple companies by this point, and I was terrified of this venture – I was ACUTELY aware of my specific inexperience. However, I did what I always did, in good times and bad… I took one step at a time and figured it out as I went along.

- Sometimes you find yourself faced with a desire to do something, but you still focus on all of the things that you DON'T have, like experience, money, and qualifications. However, there are always two ways of looking at things. I didn't know how to run a not-for-profit company, but I DID know how to launch a business. I didn't have any formal youth development qualifications, but I DID have bucketloads of lived experience of what did and didn't work from a different perspective. I didn't have any experience of working in a formal educational institution, but

I DID have a strong HR, coaching, and training background that enabled me to move people into work. And I didn't have any money to launch the business, but I DID know how to start a business on a shoestring. I didn't realise it at the time, but there were very few other people who had my specific mix of skills, which made me so uniquely poised to take on this innovative venture. All of my past experiences had developed me to the point where I was by far the most suitable person to take on this challenge. Even though at the time I felt like I had jumped around throughout my career.

CHAPTER 19

I Need to Talk to You

Since clarifying my thoughts on the youth development concept, it was like someone had lit my inner furnace again. I felt like all of a sudden I was living with a purpose. It wasn't a purpose I was able to make happen right now, but I was convinced it was definitely going to happen.

And I guess that whatever had shifted inside had also shifted something on the outside, because I ended up having more creative and inspired conversations with clients and contacts, and amazing pieces of work started falling into my lap.

I received an email from a training company I did freelance work for, asking if I could help with a piece of work they were pitching for. They recognised that it wasn't exactly the kind of thing they usually asked me to get involved with, but it was complicated. They knew I liked a challenge, and had stage experience (from my one-time stand-up comedy!), so would I be interested in designing and delivering volunteer training to a room of 800 people... 16 times over four weeks... in arenas in different cities... for a large cycling tournament that was having one of its legs in the UK!

I figuratively shit a brick.

That was, without a doubt, way out of my league. But then again, who the fuck *would* be able to turn around and say that was exactly up their street? So, I did what I always did: I took a deep breath and threw my hat in the ring.

To this day, that contract has been one of the most exhilarating and exhausting experiences of my life. I had microphone wires threaded in places that hadn't been touched in months (I'd lost the will to date again!), the team looked to me to lead on engaging the audience, I had attendees come up to me after and ask for selfies and autographs as a memoir of the experience, and I even had 1.5 seconds of TV coverage on BBC North Yorkshire!

And all the way through, I felt like I didn't deserve to be there. That I was making it up as I went along. And that at some point, someone would "find me out" and ask me to leave. That was a feeling I had become accustomed to, though, and one which I had learnt over the years to park on the sidelines and instead trust in the reactions in front of me to gauge whether it was valid or not. So, I carried on regardless, and it sparked in me an interest in something that would go on to be the first step on a very long ladder… up.

I also stumbled across a completely random piece of work. I was having dinner with a friend of a friend, talking about projects where we felt we had done things that were completely outside of our natural skill sets, when I mentioned doing the user guides for the systems

I had helped develop back in my admin job. One thing led to another, and within a couple of months I was on a plane to Sweden to help one of their suppliers re-write the user guide for a piece of heavy machinery that automated spreading tarmac on roads. It was a hugely expensive piece of machinery, and they needed someone to re-write the manual, but also to design and run an accredited train-the-trainer course for its future users.

I, of course, was no tarmacker. I also often struggled to reverse my 4x4 into parking spaces, so was unlikely to be adept at operating heavy machinery. However, it would appear that the combination of the skills of writing manuals, designing training, developing assessment frameworks, selecting potential operators, delivering training, and training technical assessors, was something that not many other people possessed. So, although I hadn't done this kind of project before, I had covered each of the different elements across my career; once again, I took a deep breath and threw my hat in the ring. I figured that all specialists start with a project they've never done before – otherwise, they could never learn.

And that's how I spent the next couple of months – working away from home, learning how to operate the machine, shut away in my office designing everything, and travelling around to deliver the course.

I had again become a bit of a nomad, living out of a suitcase, but this time I didn't mind it so much because I had pretty much come to the conclusion that if I couldn't get funding to get The Platform Project off the ground, I would put the money in myself. It's what you would do if it was a profit-making business, and this was no different really. The fact that delivering this tarmac machine project would bring significant financial benefits, was enough to keep me going.

I spent the majority of the tail end of 2015 travelling away, thrusting my dog onto my trusty dog-sitter (my mum), who I barely had the time to see in-between all my work commitments. I had, however, recognised my need for a break, so booked a 10-day holiday to go and visit my friend, Julie, for New Year in Canada, where she had moved after meeting her husband.

On Christmas Eve, I picked my mum up to stay at my house for a few days over Christmas. She insisted on doing the cooking for a good reason – I have many skills, but they don't really lie in the kitchen! On our way back to my house, we had to do the obligatory stop at seven million shops to pick up every last thing we could possibly want to consume over the next two days.

It was 5pm by the time we got back to the house, and after unpacking the car, playing Tetris in the fridge in an attempt to try and fit everything in, wrapping my brother's presents – he was a fireman on shifts at the time, and would be coming home at 10am on Christmas morning – I couldn't be arsed to go out for the usual Christmas Eve drinks with my old school friends. I text them my apologies, and put on my fleecy pyjamas to settle down for the night watching a crappy movie with Mum.

I poured us both an oversized glass of wine, and sank

down on my sofa next to her. "I'm glad you didn't go out tonight," she said. "I need to talk to you."

I took a big sip of my wine glass, steadying myself for the talk I knew had been coming. No doubt, it would be along the lines of me having neglected my responsibilities as a dog owner, or not spending enough time with Mum, or to be careful I didn't burn myself out again… yada yada.

"I have lung cancer."

CHAPTER LESSONS:

- Appreciate every moment you can spend with your loved ones, because you never know when they won't be there any more.

CHAPTER 20

The End of Life As I Knew It

I nearly choked on my wine. Mum had always had a habit of wanting to talk about death and funeral plans at Christmastime…

"What?" I said with a slight laugh and nervous half smile…

"I found out a couple of weeks ago," she replied. "I don't know how bad it is. I haven't met with a consultant yet. But I've already decided I'm not having treatment. If this is my time, then so be it," she said indignantly, true to form as ever.

I didn't know what to say. You know that it's common – 1-in-3 and all that – but you never expect to have that conversation yourself.

We spent the next few hours talking, about what I don't know, but the time flew. She showed me her medication and we worked out how much morphine she should be taking. It turned out she had been in pain for quite a while.

After we talked, we didn't know what else to do. I

didn't want to go to bed. I wanted to spend as much time with her as possible, so we did the typically British thing – and put a movie on rather than talk about the scary possibilities of her diagnosis.

After the film finished, we discussed how we would tell my brother. She didn't want to tell him on Christmas Day, but I said that he would never forgive either of us if he found out we had both sat there knowing without telling him. That was also assuming we didn't give the game away, which was unlikely given that the morphine had already made her slightly incoherent.

We considered calling him then, to get him home from work. But he worked an hour away, and we would have to tell him that it was something serious for him to leave work, then he would have to drive an hour's journey whilst distracted. So, we decided the least unfavourable option was to tell him when he got home in the morning.

I went to bed and Googled everything there was to know about lung cancer, then cried myself to sleep at the thought of losing my best friend.

In the morning, I awoke with the expectedly puffy eyes. I just wanted to curl up into a familiar ball and wait for this to pass, but I knew it wouldn't. And although it was the last thing I wanted to do, I figured that if this was probably the last Christmas we would have together, I wanted the photographs to be nice (or as nice as possible!), so I did my best to do my hair and makeup, and put some proper clothes on.

Mum was still sleeping, so I gave her a gentle poke and she awoke – still groggy. I asked if she wanted a cup of tea, to which she said, "Yes, with gin please." I wasn't sure if that was a joke, a serious request, or a morphine-induced Freudian slip.

By 10am, we were both sitting at the kitchen table, staring at each other, watching the clock. Then we heard the knock at the door and looked at each other pensively. I let my brother in, and he beamed at me. "Happy Christmas!" he said while he hugged me, and then walked over to Mum, arms out to do the same.

"I have lung cancer," she blurted out.

I guess she didn't know how to do it any more elegantly or well-timed than that. But I suppose there is no good way to tell your kids you're dying. Like me, my brother hugged her in a weird kind of delayed reaction, with the same nervous half laugh as he replied, "What?"

We stumbled through Christmas Day on autopilot. Mum was increasingly groggy and incoherent from the morphine, and sat at the dining table, half conscious, as Rhys and I cooked Christmas dinner. We could barely look at each other for fear of falling apart and ruining what might be our last Christmas together.

We pulled crackers and took some nice selfies, just like any other normal Christmas Day. Then, after dinner, we embraced the elephant in the room. We discussed what she did know, which wasn't a lot. She had struggled with her breathing over the past year or two, and had gotten noticeably slower when walking,

190

etc, but we had all put that down to her COPD lung disease, which was related to her lifelong smoking habit. She had an appointment booked with a consultant at the hospital on New Year's Eve, and then would know more about treatment options, which we talked her into at least considering.

I was resolute that I would not be going to Canada for my holiday on the 28th. She was equally resolute that if I didn't go, she wouldn't let either of us go to her appointment with her. So there was no reason to stay, I couldn't do anything in the meantime anyway, and it was only for ten days. I begrudgingly agreed, and we continued our Christmas routine as normally as we could.

The morning of my departure came, and I dropped my dog off at Mum's. She gave me a kiss on the cheek, and asked if I could fix something before I left. She handed me the lid of her inhaler and a compact mirror I had bought her for Christmas. She was clearly confused but got angry when I asked how much morphine she had had. I said I wasn't going to Canada because she needed help, and she got angry, telling me that this was her journey and that I needed to stop mollycoddling her. The last thing I wanted was to fall out with her, so I begrudgingly agreed to go, and called my brother on the way to the airport to make sure he would regularly check in on her.

I checked in for my flight with a sense of unease, but my brother assured me that he had everything in hand.

When I arrived in Canada, I immediately told my friend about Mum's news so that she would understand if I appeared distracted. She reassured me by explaining that her mum had had cancer, and had fully recovered since. I felt slightly better about the situation, and we spent the next few days shopping, sightseeing, and playing with her new-born baby. Then the day of the 31st came around, and Mum's appointment.

As the UK is usually about five hours ahead of Canada, I had set my alarm for the early hours of the morning so that I could speak to my brother and find out what the consultant had said.

He was struggling to speak. "We went to the appointment and they admitted her straight away because of her confusion. They say she has weeks rather than months... The consultant said you should come home," he managed to squeeze out between his sniffs.

I was silent for a while, then snapped out of it and said ok. I hung up with tears in my eyes, and immediately called British Airways to see if I could change my flights. Thanks to a kind lady at the customer services desk, who bent a few rules, I was on a flight just as the Canadian New Year came in.

The minute the plane landed, I called my brother.

"You need to prepare yourself, Sadie," he told me. "She's not in a good way. I had to come back again during the night because she was threatening to kill one of the orderlies; she thinks they are keeping her prisoner.

She's so confused she doesn't even know where she is, so they've had to sedate her."

I bit back the tears as I drove home, picked up a small bag of things (I wasn't planning on leaving the hospital once I got there), and found a space in the hospital car park.

As I walked into the ward, I could see my brother sitting next to a bed, looking like he had aged twenty years. He smiled at me numbly when I arrived, and gave me an update. They were about to move her to a private room so we could have some privacy, which was a clear sign that they didn't hold out much hope. Mum was unconscious, yet looked comfortable. But she bore very little resemblance to the woman I had seen just the week before; her grey skin looked almost iridescent.

I told my brother he could go and freshen up and, although he clearly felt guilty about leaving, he was grateful for the offer, and darted out of the building. Poor sod – he'd basically had to cope with all of this on his own.

I kicked myself for going to Canada. Maybe if I had stayed, I could have spotted signs of early decline sooner? Or at least been there to help Rhys? I sat at Mum's bedside and waited. There didn't seem much else I could do.

A few hours later, they moved her to her own room, and my other brother Oz arrived. The night consultant came and visited us, telling us that it was a very aggressive type of cancer, and that her confusion was caused by a mix of a bladder infection and too much morphine in her system, which was caused by her unusually low level of oxygen and metabolism. Or it sounded something like that; in truth, it was all a bit of a blur. He said they would put her on drugs to fight the infection and see what her response was like tomorrow. So, I slept in the chair and waited.

In the morning, I awoke to Mum coughing. She was coming round, so I grabbed her some water and a straw. She seemed more coherent, so I asked if she knew where she was, and why she was there. She didn't.

I had to tell my mother that she had cancer... and she took it like it was the first time she had ever heard the news. Pragmatic as ever, though, she told me that it was about time I learnt to do my own ironing!

The doctors were hopeful at her positive response to the drugs, so the three of us called round family and friends to tell them of the news and to see if a few she had asked for could visit. They did, and there were actually moments where we all laughed, sharing stories and making jokes about her going to severe lengths to get out of cooking Sunday roast for us, or her not being able to resist still picking my brother up on his overuse of the filler word 'like' in sentences. Sadly, her eldest son from her first marriage declined our invitation, which made me realise that even in the darkest moments of life, some people still hold onto their wounds above all else.

I'm glad we had that day, because it was the last day we ever saw our mother as any semblance of the woman we knew. The next day, she became confused again;

the day after, incoherent; and the day after that, barely conscious other than for us to feed her the occasional yoghurt and her to respond with single syllable words.

My two brothers and I pulled shifts, making sure that one of us was with her twenty-four hours a day. She was in hospital for one week before passing away during one of our handovers. All three of us said our final farewells at 5pm on Friday, 8th January, 2016.

I switched into autopilot for the next month. I had decided that I wanted to plan her funeral. Mum had never been a saver, so didn't have a funeral plan arranged, and I figured it would provide me with a distraction which would also enable to me exercise my control-freak tendencies and make sure we didn't end up with a generic service.

I set about arranging a date – five weeks' time, on a Friday afternoon, so that all of her relatives from Wales could come, and my nieces could visit from Germany. I booked the crematorium, and reverted to form by writing a project plan for the to-do list!

I called around a number of funeral agents, most of whom told me either that "I should be grieving and leave all this up to the professionals who knew what they were doing" or that I was "being unrealistic" in my expectations of what they would and wouldn't do. I basically just wanted them to arrange "storage and transport" (a horrible description, but there was no other way of putting it!) while I took care of the service. Most, though, refused to just do the low value bits.

Their insistence that I couldn't do it on my own made me even more determined to prove them wrong. I persevered and kept calling round until I found one beautifully kind-hearted and caringly accommodating independent firm, who said they would basically do whatever I needed of them. And they charged me the minimal price, knowing that I had to find the money from my own pocket. It was yet another example that there is good in the world – you just sometimes have to push past the nay-sayers to find it.

The service was beautiful, and I even managed to hold it together long enough to deliver the eulogy.

Then, it was back to reality with a bump.

All of a sudden, I didn't have the service planning to distract me, and there was a gaping hole in my life that I had no idea how (or desire) to fill. I would regularly have random waves of tears, which meant that I had to keep my driving to a minimum, and I could feel the familiar dark edges of depression creeping towards me.

Then I received an email. A company related to the one I had done the tarmacking project for had a big change project they needed managing, in a very short space of time. It would basically require me to move up to Nottingham for six months, and they wanted to know if I was interested. Although I knew that it wouldn't fix the void in my life, I desperately needed a distraction. I wasn't ready to go back to my normal life without her in it yet, so I took the contract.

It didn't make the pain go away, but it did give me time

to adjust while I found my feet with a new life routine. Instead of calling her every day, I began phoning friends instead. Rather than going to Mum's for Sunday lunch, I would instead go out for a drink on a Sunday evening with my dad. Ever so slowly, bit by bit, I reconstituted my life in a way that didn't seem too painful to live in. And after I finished that contract, I took another one.

I was ready to live my life again, but I wasn't sure what I wanted that life to look like. The Platform Project had become a distant thought while I had settled into the lifestyle of a contractor, and the money and opportunities ahead of me were familiar coping strategies/addictively-numbing distractions!

I do recognise that taking that contract was me running away. But I also recognise that had I not, my life wouldn't have ended up taking the amazing turn it did over the following couple of years.

CHAPTER LESSONS:

- When you know your final moments with loved ones are finite, all you do is focus on the moments you have wasted. Those weekends you skipped out on with a shitty excuse. Those stupid arguments you had over nothing. Those times when you begrudged taking them to the supermarket because you had far better things to be doing. Why is it that things only seem to become valuable when they are in short supply?

- I struggled to adjust to Mum's passing because she had been such a big part of my daily life. But as time passed, I learnt to adjust and cope with that sense of loss. The one thing that surprised me, though, was that as much as I had the standard sense of regret of the small moments together I had squandered away, I didn't have an overwhelming sense of regret as my brothers did, because I had built such a close relationship with her. You can't change your relationship with loved ones after they are gone, but always try and remember that although you may have other things you need to be doing in those moments that seem so important at the time, you won't even remember what they were when looking back from their deathbed.

CHAPTER 21

Re-launch

My foray back into consulting resulted in me deciding to merge my business with a project management consultancy I had worked with on the previous two projects. There were a lot of opportunities ahead of us, and it made sense to merge my organisational design background with their project management disciplines to manage bigger company transformation projects.

There was just one problem... When we won new work, my heart sank rather than sang. The time had come where I yet again felt trapped. However, this time, rather than see it as a failure or that I had taken the wrong pathway, I recognised it for what it was... it was a decision that was right for me at the time, and it had served its purpose. Namely, to make me realise that although I was good at this stuff, it was not what I wanted to be doing as my main focus.

About two years after Mum died, my world seemed to be re-stabilising, and I felt it was time to re-launch The Platform Project.

However, I was also aware that I needed to earn a living on the side. Although I could sell my shares in the merged company, it wouldn't sustain my current level of living, which was aligned to an expensive contractors' life! And I was conscious I didn't just want to go back to doing what I had been doing before. I needed some help to figure out what I DID want to do. It felt like something inside me had shifted since Mum's death, but I couldn't put my finger on it, or what it meant for my future.

So, I engaged the services of a coach to help me figure it out. I had had a few different coaches over the years at different stages of my life. One just after I started up in business, to help me figure my way and maintain momentum. One just after my breakdown, to help me maintain my self-care. And one now, who I chose because I wanted help to figure out who I was and what I wanted.

At our first session, I sat in the chair with my notepad and pen, as I always did with my action-focused coaching sessions. Then she told me that I wouldn't need any paper for these sessions – they were about BEING, not DOING, and I should close my eyes. *Oh, my God*, I thought to myself. *I'm gonna have to find another coach, aren't I?! This is ridiculous.* But I followed instructions to be polite and humour her… and after six sessions of tears, revelations, and a deep level of understanding I didn't even think possible, I came out the other side feeling like a changed person.

I went in wanting to do things like write a book, publish articles, speak about my experiences, and inspire the world to change... but feeling like I had no right or capability to do so. I realised that my armour had served me well to get me to that point, but was now standing in front of me, blocking my way.

I couldn't do any of these things unless I did them as my true authentic self. And until I embraced the fact that every choice, every decision, and every fuck-up I had made in my journey to this point placed me in the perfect position to do these things as *me*.

At some point along my journey, I had graduated from being some wannabe, young, pretend professional that hid behind a suit of armour, to a daring, heart-led entrepreneur that had at some point not just grown into the shoes she felt she was playing dress-up in, but actually outgrown them.

When I had my breakdown, I felt like I had fallen off my pedestal, whereas I hadn't realised until now that I was actually on the wrong fucking pedestal! It's clearly not something I would recommend people should do, but I now realised that having my breakdown was actually the best thing that could have happened to me. Although it took me a few years to sort my shit out, and several side-tracked events that nearly sucked me back in, for the first time EVER I actually felt like me, carving my own path, achieving the things that were important to ME.

With this new-found clarity in mind, I set about taking some substantial actions, the first of which was to say goodbye to two decades as a little blonde imposter... and replace it with the same shade of fiery red that my mum sported in her heyday. Dying my hair was, of course, only a cosmetic change, but for me, at that moment, it felt like a symbolic change that said, "Hello world… this is me, and I'm not afraid to be seen!" It was like I had stepped into my superwoman outfit, and I was ready for action. So then, and only then, did I start making some proper changes.

I downsized my finances to a quarter of my previous outgoings. The flashy car went, the extortionate holidays disappeared, and the shopping stopped. My outgoings reduced to the extent that the bank actually called to check I was ok!

I re-mortgaged and rented out my spare rooms for some extra income, which meant I was now a 35-year-old living with strangers. But it was a means to an end, and placed me in a position where I didn't have to take paid work more than two days a week whilst I re-launched the project.

I set out to re-establish the youth development contacts I had made a few years earlier, apologising for the delay, but explaining that I was now in a position where I could proceed.

And I (temporarily!) downsized my ambitions for the project to get it off the ground. So, rather than a 'full-size model', I launched it as a pilot to test the market. I put £2k of my own money in to cover the set-up costs, found a couple of volunteers who were willing to muddle through with me, and a small local community venue. Then we ran a week-long youth enterprise challenge during the August school holidays, where teenagers would be researching, designing, and pitching a range of printed goods (t-shirts, phone covers, mugs and inspirational wall signs, etc).

Many of the people I spoke to doubted I would get referrals from established agencies like schools and youth agencies because I wasn't established... but we did. Almost all of them doubted that the participants would give up five full days of their summer holiday time... but they did. Everyone doubted it would work with a group of mixed, unknown, high-needs, differently-aged young people... but it did. And we had no idea whether they would interact well with external business professionals coming in to share their story and teach their skills. But they did!

At every turn, we were astounded at the results we were seeing. Confidence was boosted. Engagement was increased. Attendance was high. Teamworking was developed. Relationships were formed. Aspirations were raised. And outcomes were achieved, in that ALL of the initial group of six went on to re-engage with education, get a job, or actually start their own sideline business. After just ONE week's involvement!

I had hoped it would work, but I'd had no idea it would be that effective. So, we built on that and ran a further seven challenges over the next year – some as open challenges; some over longer periods; and some 'in-house', for schools that wanted help with specific groups of children. We received some funding to run innovative, daring projects on entrepreneurial skills and social enterprise causes, and our numbers kept increasing.

We were then chosen by Nationwide as part of an innovation strategic partnership, as they wanted to help us scale the project. And since then, we have really raised our sights. The first year was about testing whether we really could teach young people entrepreneurial skills in short, sharp challenges.

Now, our goal over the next couple of years is to develop the 'full-scale' undertaking, which would be an alternative to college or work, and look something like a hybrid 'training workplace'. Participants would learn how to be self-employed and run their own business by actually managing one of a few (real, trading) differently-themed youth enterprises in a shared workspace, under the guidance of a range of youth workers, professional skills specialists, and community business partnerships.

Just imagine: it would be a bit like one of those shared office buildings, where you have multiple businesses working under the same roof. Only these businesses would be 'owned' by the project as a real 'live' skills incubation space, all run as not-for-profits, and managed by young people with the support of skills specialists, who could then support them to launch their own business or a find a job when they discover what they love doing.

This is a really experimental model, and a bold, ballsy move, because it's basically saying that the established approach to developing young people for work is becoming less and less future-proof, and seeing more and more young people falling through the cracks. And as with all good experiments, I still have no idea exactly what it's going to look like and I am sure it will evolve over time, but I do know that the vision is strong, and my intention to make it work is even stronger.

That is why I am now speaking at conferences and events to help other schools, colleges, training providers, and workplaces learn how to embrace some of the concepts that we have leveraged in order to help their young people develop more entrepreneurial skills. And I'm loving every moment of it.

Public speaking wouldn't have been part of my new model if it weren't for my coaching experience with Sarah. Only one year ago, I still felt like I didn't have the gravitas or experience to offer a statement for a local newspaper article, let alone stand on a stage and 'preach' to a bunch of experienced professionals about how to do what they have been doing for decades. But what I realised was that my LACK OF EXPERIENCE in that specific field is what gave me fresh insight and different ideas. The power of my inexperience is what has carried me forward at every stage of my career.

It's why my early clients listened to me – because I wasn't blinded by the things that they had seen too many times to see them clearly any more. It was why I could train rooms full of professionals – because I used it to simplify what was underneath what they felt were complex people issues. And it was why I always evolved my way out of partnerships – because I wanted to learn so badly that once I had mastered something, I needed to move on. If I knew how to do something, it meant I had done it already, and was therefore standing still.

This is the realisation that led me to dump my armour and, in the words of Brene Brown, "lean into my vulnerability". Being daring and courageous means that you HAVE TO feel like you are out of your depth most of the time, because there are no guarantees when you put yourself out there.

And that's now what I'm doing. I'm working on The Platform Project pretty much full-time to grow it, whilst still taking the occasional bit of training, consultancy, and speaking work, when something that interests me comes along. I'm occasionally writing for publications, provoking changes to established thinking in the world of education and corporate practice, and no longer giving a fuck whether anyone disagrees with me. I'm standing on stages and openly admitting that I still feel like I make it up as I go along, but without that sense of inadequacy. And I'm writing this book – exposing all of my chinks and rough edges – with no fear (ok, maybe just a little) that it might go down like a shit sandwich.

So, this is me – from broken to best, despite the odds, using all of my knocks to propel me forward to a place I never thought possible.

Life is inviting me to step up, and I'm using my lifelong lessons as the rungs on the ladder.

Will you do the same?

THE END… or just the beginning of the next chapter?

About the Author

After graduating from law school and realising that her lack of attention to detail would probably be a bit career limiting(!), Sadie made an early start in the world of management consultancy at the tender age of 22, using what little legal knowledge she had to tell small companies why they couldn't fire people! Then, after a whole 18 months of experience and a shed-load of youthful naivety, she decided to go it alone and set up her first consultancy business at 24. Since then, Sadie Sharp has been one of the youngest freelance female management consultants in the UK, working with a range of large organisations across the world.

Over the past 10+ years, she has started 5+ companies, coached CEOs, trained over 10,000 managers, spoken in front of audiences of 800+ people, done stand-up comedy, and launched a trailblazing youth development social enterprise. During that time, she has also gone into business with the wrong partners, fired everyone and started from scratch, suffered from a breakdown and depression, and lost her mother to cancer in less than two weeks.

Sadie now spends most of her time growing her not-for-profit youth development company, The Platform Project, to create a generation of young entrepreneurs, as well as living her mission in life to help everyone else embrace their insecurities and do the things their smaller selves would only dream of.

For any queries about Sadie's training, coaching, writing or speaking services, please visit:

www.SadieSharp.co.uk

And Sadie genuinely LOVES hearing any stories and feedback about how this book might have resonated with you, so please do send in your comments through the website Contact Us form, and leave a review on Amazon to help the book get out there and transform other lives.

Printed in Poland
by Amazon Fulfillment
Poland Sp. z o.o., Wrocław

54349165R00125